P9-DHS-481

BATHROOM DESIGN

BATHROOM DESIGN

BARRY DEAN

SIMON AND SCHUSTER · NEW YORK

Copyright © 1985 Smallwood & Stewart

All rights reserved including the right of
reproduction in whole or in part in any form.

Published by Simon and Schuster
A Division of Simon & Schuster, Inc.
Simon & Schuster Building
Rockefeller Center
1230 Avenue of the Americas
New York, New York 10020

SIMON AND SCHUSTER
and colophon are registered
trademarks of Simon & Schuster, Inc.

Library of Congress Cataloging
in Publication Data

Dean, Barry.
Bathroom design.

Includes index.
1. Bathrooms. 2. Interior decoration. I. Title.
NK2117.B33D43   1985   728   85-14289
ISBN: 0-671-55203-1

Produced by Smallwood & Stewart,
6 Alconbury Road, London E.5.

Designed by Marjorie Katz Design Inc.

Printed and bound in Italy
by New Interlitho S.P.A., Milan

First Edition
1 2 3 4 5 6 7 8 9 10

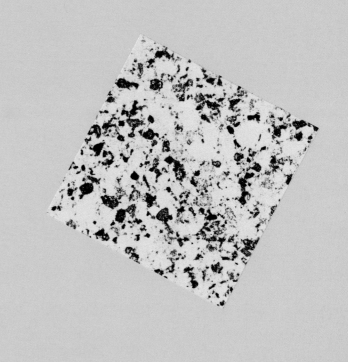

CONTENTS

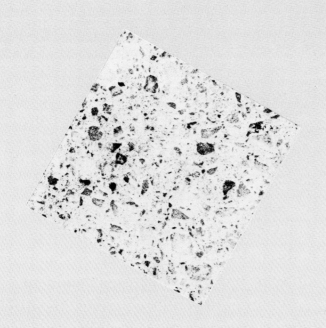

INTRODUCTION
8

SURVEY OF
STYLE
11

DESIGN FOR
PURPOSE
53

Family Bathrooms
Bathrooms for Couples
Master Bathrooms
Bed and Bath
Small Bathrooms
Children's Bathrooms
Bathrooms for the Disabled
Second Bathrooms
Exercise Bathrooms
Indoor-Outdoor Bathrooms

THE
ESSENTIALS
95

Sinks and Faucets
Toilets and Bidets
Showers and Steambaths
Saunas
Bathtubs
Whirlpools and Hot Tubs

DESIGN
DETAILS
121

Lighting
Walls
Floors
Storage
Mirrors
Windows

DESIGN
DIRECTORY
155

WORKING
WITH A
PROFESSIONAL
181

INDEX
188
CREDITS
190
ACKNOWLEDGEMENTS
192

INTRODUCTION

The most cheerless room in the house, yet the one which influences the opening and close of our day; the least intimate room in the house, yet the place where we perform our most personal hygiene and grooming; the most recent addition to the house, but in many respects the most backward-looking: the modern bathroom is an anachronism but one so universal and familiar that it barely raises comment.

Yet for all its contradictions this former orphan of interior design is now changing more rapidly and more radically than any other room in the house. As our attitudes to bathing are evolving, so the role of the bathroom is expanding. The solitary privy is merging with other rooms to become an indoor-outdoor spa, an exercise area, or simply a comfortable, expansive refuge for relaxation and seclusion (the bathroom is still the only room in the house where one can demand privacy). In each case the new concept of the bathroom is presenting architects and designers with challenges that are all the more exciting and demanding because they have no recent precedent.

In some respects this book is a visual documentary of many of the most imaginative and stylish approaches to the bathroom in all its forms, new and old. The diverse and sometimes divergent personalities and designs it embraces do not advocate a single style, for no one aesthetic could satisfy the variety that is the bathroom. It is rather a collection of styles and approaches which are intended as much to inspire and to stimulate as to provide a model.

This book is as much about style as it is about design for the bathroom. It is only appropriate that this most intimate room should closely reflect our personal style. Style is so varied in its expressions: one of its charms is that it is neither dictated nor measured by money or fashion. As the following pages show, its best examples are timeless, simple, and endlessly satisfying.

NEW ATTITUDES

Not only are the standard fixtures we inherited from the Victorians altering, but so are the attitudes they express. This largely reflects a new interest in personal care and health and exercise—concerns that have altered the way we live. Hot tubs led the way most visibly in the early 1970s, and whirlpools, steambaths, saunas, and exercise equipment are now appearing in bathrooms. These luxurious additions are evidence of our new view of bathing as therapeutic, both psychologically and physically, as much for simple hygiene.

The Romans appreciated this restful, reviving aspect of bathing, and the Japanese have long viewed Western bathing habits as over-simplified at best. Like that of the Finns and some other older cultures, Japanese bathing is a method of relaxation and therapy—in a sense a deeper cleansing than we ordinarily accept in the West. Of course, doctors have for many years extolled those virtues of hydrotherapy that we have voiced in more mundane terms of recommending a hot bath or a cold shower. But only now through saunas, whirlpools, and so on is it being accepted as part of everyday bathing. Indeed, perhaps it is because the bathroom has always been more heavily cloaked in euphemisms than any other room in the house that we have sometimes failed to recognize its inconsistencies and inadequacies. We can easily become insensible to the lack of comfort or character in rooms referred to by such bland genteelisms as 'powder room' or 'restroom'.

But it is our growing awareness of the importance of the design of our surroundings that will most transform and humanize the bathroom. Visible in the decorative spirit in architecture and new mood of collaboration between artists, designers, and craftspeople, evidenced in galleries and one of a kind designs, this insistence on good design promises an exciting future. Today's potent enthusiasm will do most to create the comfort sacrificed for functionalism in the bathroom and inspire the design changes to make this unique room truly practical, safer, and pyschologically healthy.

SURVEY
OF
STYLE

The Romans bathed for relaxation, refreshment, and social entertainment as much as hygiene. According to the ancient Roman poet Horace, many of his contemporaries 'recite their writings . . . while bathing'. One of the most far-flung of these public imperial spas was the Aqua Sulis at Bath, England, built in the 2nd-century A.D.

Gwathmey-Siegel translated the ancient grandeur of the imperial bath into modern forms and materials in this Long Island home. Combining clear and translucent glass block creates privacy but enables bathers to see the Atlantic Ocean.

*G*old curtains part to reveal rich bro-
cade and enhance the performance of
Roman-style ablutions at the 18th-
century Villino di Caddi di Stupinigi in
Italy. The oval marble tub in the Prin-
cess's bathroom is decorated with an imperial eagle grasping decorative swags.

*T*he tip-up basin is decorated with the head of Zeus and silvery fish.

*T*his High Victorian imperial bath was designed by John Chapple for his patron, the immensely wealthy Lord Bute. Medieval elements are freely combined here in Lady Bute's sumptuous washstand at Castle Coch, Glamorganshire. The pair of towers held containers for hot and cold water.

Sumptuous black and tan marble and lavish gilt cornices create a grandiose Italian bathroom fit for a Medici. Dull mirrored tiles cover the walls and ceiling of the bathtub area.

*V*ictorian architect William Burges designed this washstand for his own rooms in London, employing a tortoise mosaic marble. A medieval-style frieze of bathing scenes and ornate crimson and gold wood conceal two water tanks. Hot and cold water poured from a stylized dragon's mouth below.

The Victorian bath was often a celebration of the virtues of cleanliness. Here Burges combines a pastiche of styles in this deep ochre and green washstand.

Levantine marble and onyx panels cover the walls of the ladies retiring room at Harrods in London, a private club built in 1908. A pair of generous sculpted scallop basins in cream and brown striated marble flank each cubicle. The sinuous lines of the partitions are echoed in the Art Nouveau mirrors.

The formality and historical borrowings of Victorian design have been supplanted by a freer, more sensuous style. The oval and curvy adjacent mirrors reflect this new elegance.

*H*enri Sauvage designed this quintes-
*s*ential Art Nouveau bath in 1902, with
a central sunken tub and walls of a lim-
*p*id watered aquamarine. Colored light
*f*rom the large stained glass window
*w*ould bathe the entire room.

Built in the 1920s, this fairy tale bath near Oakland, California, is a celebration of Art Nouveau in its fullest bloom created at the very time the movement was losing favor. The tub area is inlaid with charmingly irregular handmade terra cotta tiles.

*F*airy tale gothic animal details are repeated throughout. The dolphin waterspout is an exquisite example of decorative exuberance, while in a corner the basin opens like a delicate buttercup on a jade green pedestal stem.

In dancer Tilly Losch's bathroom (1932), English artist and designer Paul Nash employed only severely right-angled lines with the single exception of parenthetical semicircles of neon tube lighting. Every flat surface is faced with black stippled glass, giving the room an appearance of shimmering motion.

*N*ash espoused a new aesthetic that would take advantage of machine production: "The factory must adapt itself to the artist and not the other way around". His bathroom design was lavish in its use of new machine-age materials. The walls are sheets of black and deep purple glass, the ceiling black marmarate glass, and the floor pink rubber. Neon tube lighting surrounds the sink.

This elegant bath in Standford Hall, Leicestershire looks like tomorrow but was actually executed in 1928. The opulence is understated in that all unnecessary adornment has been eliminated. The sunken white marble tub is big enough to swim a few strokes in, and both light and water pour from the boy astride the conch shell.

The hall-of-mirrors effect in this 1930s bath is reminiscent of the style of Syrie Maugham: dignified in its use of the classical and yet unabashedly magnificent. Water pours forth from the mouth of a Romanesque dolphin. The sink is set into a marble mantle-like affair, and an onyx dado and black marble banding keep the room from going out into mirrored infinity.

The timeless style of these faucets belies the fact that they were installed in 1937 by designers White Allom for the guest bathroom in Eltham Palace in England. Most likely they were manufactured by Crane in the United States.

Red marble surrounds the tub set majestically between the twin fluted pillars in this Art Deco bath in Regents Park, London. Designer Robert Lutyens eliminated all unnecessary details and those remaining have been spared no expense. The domed light conceals air vents around its lip; the fluted pilasters are mirrored.

A sumptuous Persian carpet, dark wood-sided tub, and generous oval pedestal sink provide casual elegance appropriate to this room's ample dimensions.

The Brussels apartment of René and Barbara Stoeltie fairly flaunts High Thirties style. Resplendent in midnight blue and white Belgium marble, the geometric mystique of Art Deco appears in the bathroom window, door panes, and ceiling light.

The curvilinear line and the personal object are lavishly used in this bath in Provence. French windows open onto a balcony for delicate morning light.

The medieval bath was a resplendent affair complete with banquets served on floating trays. This bath in a 14th-century Italian castle, reconstructed by Piero Pinto for designer Laura Biagiotti, is lacking only the banquet. It is authentically medieval down to the aged terra cotta tiles.

In a converted Los Angeles warehouse Eve Steele created this minimalist bathroom adjoining her dressing room. Concrete treated with an industrial water sealant covers the walls and framed-out bath.

Beneath the wooden eaves of a French farmhouse this sun-filled bath includes skirted twin sinks and a modern sunken tub with a grand approach.

By day this early Renaissance bath-with-a-view is lit with reflected Mediterranean sunlight, and at night by the glowing electric candelabra in a villa designed by 15th-century architect Falconetto.

*G*auze blinds admit a limpid light into this modern version of the traditional bed and bath. Green neon tubing replaces the ceiling molding.

*O*utdoor and indoor are blended in this modern geometric aesthetic. California architect Mel Bernstein's measured plan for this multi-purpose space is everywhere softened by an exuberant use of color.

This vacation house on the windswept volcanic island of Pantelleria, off the coast of Italy, captures the Homeric spirit of its location. Austere and imposing, the outdoors is drawn indoors, and the ancient black rock of the hillside becomes the bathroom wall.

*C*ube-shaped lights crown four polished marble columns in François Catroux's fantasia bath for the annual Salon des Artistes Décorateurs in Paris. The shower employs a waterfall effect instead of the usual single jet stream.

*M*irrors behind the massive slant-sided gray marble tub make it appear to float mid-room. The towels and upholstery are custom-made by Porthault.

*I*n keeping with their belief in the therapeutic values of bathing, the Japanese create tranquil environments for their soaking tubs. Chicago architect Michael Lustig recreated this harmonious atmosphere with traditional aged maki wood and luminous silk shoji screens.

*F*unctional simplicity belies the luxury of this custom-designed, marble-edged soaking pool in a California bed-bath. Underlining the drama of its center stage position are the bright red steps.

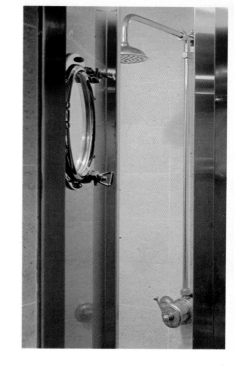

*H*aving gone to the limits of High Tech in his previous quarters, fashion designer Joseph choose Eva Jiricna's minimal design for his London flat. Cool cream marble and polished stainless steel explore the aesthetics of understatement.

*T*he shower stall is of burnished steel, as are the sink and hospital bath. Finding locks and handles 'too clumsy' for the sleek environment, Joseph eliminated them. On the wall is the satellite mirror by Eileen Gray.

This minimal Japanese bath cast in gray concrete was designed by Bromley-Jacobson for the Kips Bay show. The shower is lined in burnished metal, and the door shows the influence of Frank Lloyd Wright. A hot red neon skylight contrasts with the cool gray stone and industrial metalwork.

Classicism and modernism combine in this Italian post-modern treatment of the imperial spa. Mosaics and a half-finished brick wall add to the 'ruins' atmosphere. Asymmetrical details such as the legs of the crooked geometric table by Hans Hollein unexpectedly interrupt any ancient reveries.

A modern version of classical treatment is seen in this bathroom designed by Carl D'Aquino in a Beaux Arts building on lower Fifth Avenue in New York City. The owners wanted an elegant, airy, almost ethereal quality to the room which needed to function as both master bath and powder room. A floor of rose-grained French marble runs throughout, and the door picks up the rose color. White glass and plaster moldings create an illusion of expansion. Mirrors reflect the grandeur of the few well chosen neo-classical details such as the graceful marble topped oval sink and elegant shower head.

Italian designer Gianni Versace's bath in his 18th-century Villa Fontanella on the shores of Lake Como features classicism on a grand scale, true to the spirit of the house. Busts of Hercules and Minerva adorn the room; the ceiling is decorated with frescoes of birds; the sandstone walls are a serene blue; and the bench is of pure white Carrara marble.

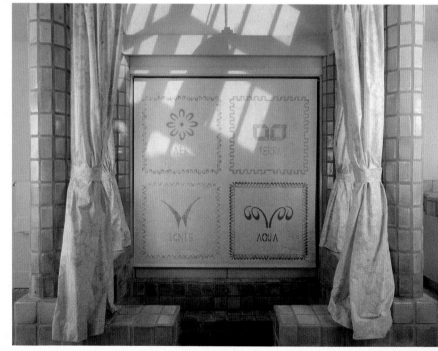

Jencks uses the post-modern symbol of the cleft pediment over the twin sinks. The mirror profiles facing out Gemini-like, fist towel holders, and repetition of symbols are all representative of Jencks's crusade against what he calls the "mindless elegance" of modernism.

Charles Jencks, who christened the post-modern style, designed his Los Angeles home with Moore-Yudell in four pavilions, each representing one of the ancient symbols of the four elements. In the AER pavilion, bedroom and bath open onto a pool in the shape of the state of California. The step-down tub is lined in cerulean blue tile and decorated with a stencilled frieze of the elements by Sidney Hurwitz.

An undesirable view of a California freeway was cleverly masked by architect Eric Moss in this rooftop bath house. He took the archetypal pyramid roof, and exploded and opened it up to let in sunlight. The "petal" triangles screen out all but the greenery. A fire ladder allows access from the pool below to the tub without entering the house. Railings are nylon ropes criss-crossed in shoelace fashion.

In contrast to the ultra-urban setting of the "petal house" is this sumptuously verdant courtyard bath in Bali. Tropical foliage, a thatched roof, and a slatted roll-up screen shade the bather from the intensity of the sun. The tiled tub is set in stone, as is the courtyard area. The high wall ensures privacy. The Indonesian sculpture is adorned with red hibiscus flowers, while other elements are cool in tone and texture.

DESIGN
FOR
PURPOSE

FAMILY
BATHROOMS

For centuries, family-style bathing has gone on in Japan in the *furo*, or soaking tub. The washing and soaking in the furo are public, while activities in the *benjo*, or toilet, are always discreetly separate or private. In the West, until the spread of indoor plumbing, bathing privately was a luxury only the very rich could afford. Victorian ethics then encouraged a sense of privacy that is bequeathed to us today in the single bathroom household.

A true family bathroom is rarely encountered. The most conventional solution for families is to create one master bath and a second bathroom or two. But in many apartments or smaller houses this simply isn't possible, and a well-designed family bathroom can fulfill everyone's needs.

Space should obviously be generous, both to accommodate the requirements of several users and more importantly to allow for privacy between different areas. Frequently floor space for an extra shower or sink or toilet can be gained by appropriating an adjoining room or closet. A more radical solution is to separate the toilet entirely into a private chamber.

Toilet, tub, and shower will all do singly, but installing two or even three sinks to share the load will mean a more functional room. Equally important is the exact layout of the fixtures. Plumbing constraints frequently dictate a linear arrangement of fixtures, so that connections, drains, and vents can most economically be hooked into. But a dividing wall that separates washing area from toilet or sinks from shower/bath will increase the number of people that can use the bathroom comfortably at any one time.

Finally, a slightly trivial point but one that's often overlooked: family bathrooms, particularly when the family includes even one teenager, require good storage . . . and an endless supply of fresh towels.

A wood-panelled tub and cane towel rail underline the traditionalism and sense of family history that gaze down from the walls of this London flat.

For their Parisian home, a Franco-Japanese family created a bathroom that reflects both their cultures. Black tile, gray slate, and wooden slats provide a functional serenity, contrasted with the acacia trees visible through the glass roof.

54

Not only twin sinks, but old fashioned roll-top twin tubs allow for bathing à deux in this bath spacious enough for even the most extended family.

FAMILY BATHROOMS

Efficient storage is vital to a heavily trafficked bathroom. Interesting storage cabinets highlight this pine-walled bath in London; they are supplemented by a mirrored corner medicine cabinet.

Antique fittings found at yard sales and auctions were installed by this large family in Connecticut. Three sinks were needed to handle the busy early morning hours.

A large picture window provides plenty of natural light in this low key, wood–beamed Connecticut bath. The tub is generous enough for two, allowing nature to be contemplated in a private setting.

Modern synthetic materials have opened up entirely new shapes and sizes for sinks. In this French bath, a trough–like sink is large enough for bathing a small child.

BATHROOMS
FOR COUPLES

The two adult-household is the most rapidly expanding segment of the population, and in the future the seven-bedroom house may come to seem as quaint as servants' quarters. Demographically, the couple's bathroom could be the wave of the future.

The most striking feature of a bathroom designed for a couple is the extent to which it can be personalized; only the master bathroom can compare in this respect. Without the constraints of having to consider guests, the limits of the design and decoration can be dictated solely by personal whim. The entire room can be swept clear of all personal elements to become a spare temple to the body with exercise equipment, sauna, perhaps a tanning lamp. Or the bathroom can be designed to serve as the sitting room or living room of the past—a place to read, relax, talk, or even watch a favorite movie. These approaches to the bathroom break from tradition to provide the kind of sanctuary that can be invaluable to a busy working couple.

At its most basic, a couple's bathroom should have two sinks, each with its own storage and set completely apart. For washing, a separate shower and tub are the most

practical means of coping with similar schedules—the kind of conflict that can strain the most stable of couples. Still, a generous walk-in shower with double shower heads serves the same purpose and has a luxury that belies its simplicity. Double-size tubs, since they require close coordination of bathing schedules, are less a solution to washing for two and more the epitome of intimate luxury that a couple's bath should embrace.

Los Angeles designer Jarrett Hedborg created this sophisticated bath, fit for a Nick and Nora Charles, in a Beverly Hills cottage. The alcove and lounge are lined with Italian marbelized wallpaper and eclectically furnished with Herman Miller chairs, Pace table, and antique kelim rug.

A throne-like bath is set between two 1930s chromium chairs, separating dressing, washing, and makeup areas in this French bathroom.

Authentic 19th-century fittings were used throughout for this bathroom in a renovated Tuscan farmhouse. Brass gooseneck faucets crown the twin pedestal sink.

BATHROOMS
FOR COUPLES

*T*win sinks are probably the nearest substitute for installing twin baths. Here a black and white checkerboard tile border unifies the open space of this couple's bath.

*P*aired closets flank the bath of this couple's pristine bathroom in Paris, providing ample and separate storage.

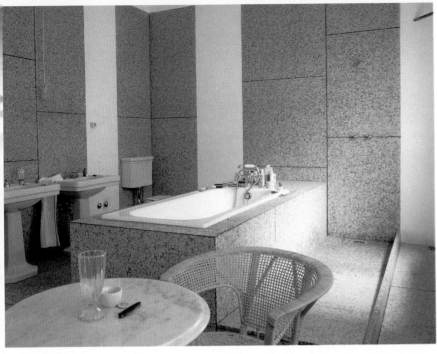

*T*he unusual absence of mirrors gives a slightly monastic feel to this wet bath lined with monumental slabs of unpolished granite. The two sinks and generous shower/bath area opening onto a larger room proclaim practicality for two.

MASTER BATHROOMS

It was Edmund Wilson who said, "I have had a good many more uplifting thoughts, creative and expansive visions—while soaking in comfortable baths or drying myself after bracing showers—in well-equipped American bathrooms than I have ever had in any cathedral." Obviously such an experience could not be had in a bathroom of mean dimensions. It requires nothing less than a master bath.

There is no more intimate room than the master bath. Its every element—scale, color, layout—is designed exactly to one person's taste, for that person alone. The room can ignore any public image to indulge completely the private personality.

Far from the rare status it suffered in past generations, the master bathroom has become a standard for most architects. In new buildings and extensions, master bed and bath suites, and even wings, include spacious walk-in closets, dressing rooms, and generous bathrooms. In existing space, closets or nearby rooms are being annexed to become master baths.

The most spacious baths include soaking tubs, saunas, and steam rooms, and may even spread the outdoors for an open-air shower or lap pool. But the real elegance of the master bath is its essence, and a tiny room can serve perfectly as well.

Delores del Rio's bath is appropriately Hollywood Deco. Her glass-topped dressing table is lit from underneath and above. The abundantly mirrored dressing area is spangled with tiny chromium stars.

*T*he decidedly masculine feeling to this master bathroom is created by the extensive use of old, rich wood. The rugged wideplank pine floor is stained to match the oak of the cabinets. The painting of the American West, handsome antique fixtures, and well organized accoutrements give the bath a gentleman's club atmosphere.

*A*n immense round mirror divides the sink and tub in this compact and cleverly designed master bath. In between, cosmetics and toiletry activity can take place on either side of the counter. Reflections open up the space while the shape of the generous sink reflects that of the mirror.

MASTER BATHROOMS

*T*his sepia French salon-cum-bath evokes
the powerful romanticism of an old photograph. Wicker chair, rose bedecked
lampshade, and potted plant, all washed
by the mellow light, make this a sanctuary where comfort and style are not
sacrificed to functionalism.

Cleanliness must approach Godliness when washing in the sanctity of the cathedral-like Gothic revival bath of Lord Bute in his castle in Cardiff, Wales. Deep-toned mahogany walls have been inset with dozens of marble panels.

This tongue-in-cheek English Victorian bathroom, fairly dripping in shawls and lace, takes romanticism to its limits. Everything is authentically Victorian, from the white cast iron claw foot tub to the summery wicker furniture, but the somber grandiloquence of the style is refreshingly absent.

BED AND BATH

The combined bed and bath becomes a cocoon, an all-purpose private area which is completely self-contained. It is economical, efficient, and with good design, a room of extraordinary visual stimulation. But successfully merging such diffuse items as shower and night table, toilet and dressing mirror, and bed with bathtub demands ingenuity, attention to detail, and painstaking planning.

The ultimate satisfaction of uniting sleeping and bathing areas is that the two most personal and intimate rooms in the home are thus conjoined. Beyond this sanctuary the public areas begin; within it the personal is truly private. The two areas of rest and relaxation, of sleeping and bathing, are therefore free to flow into one another decoratively, and some of the functional aspects of the bathroom can be humanized by the softer character of the bedroom.

The decorative treatment for bed and bath can be sleek and somber in muted neutrals, or softly gathered chintz-and-roses, a wave of white with flashes of color, airy and bright or darkly quiet. Virtually any style, and many combinations of styles, will carry the practical association of bed with bath.

There are, however, several functional requirements. The toilet is a primary consideration, as it cannot be included in the room proper. Instead, it should be contained in a separate area with a window or a closet with good ventilation. The sink and tub can be positioned with greater flexibility, but ventilation of the room should also be borne in mind to prevent conditions under which the room would fill with steam.

Any room that fills so many roles can become overpowering, and well-organized storage is essential. Built-in cupboards and closets will carry the burden of clothing and shoes, towels and toiletries, and linens. Folding screens and panels of clear or smoked glass can act as partitions when desirable.

In this iconoclastic home in Zurich designed by architect Fritz Schwartz, living, bathing, and sleeping quarters flow one into another, defined by changes of level. The bath, which lies on the other side of the sofa, has a low wall on two sides for the taps and is raised on the other to become the recess for the wash basins.

No distinction between bed and bath space is made in this old-fashioned French attic bathroom flooded with natural light. Created as a guest room, its beamed roof is painted a unifying white, as is the witty, antlered coat rack.

The bed and bath of Patrice Nourrissat in Paris introduces fantasy, and the tented bed, leopard skins, orchids, and Indo-Portuguese art are reminiscent of some sultan's quarters.

The canopy is made of reversible fabric from the 1920s. An 18th-century quilt covers the bed.

This traditional washstand seems to epitomize the unpretentious romanticism of country style. Chalk blue walls, white lace, and cool marble evoke a dreamy purity.

A no-nonsense yet romantic approach was taken in this loft bed and bath in Manhattan's SoHo district. The frankly industrial setting is underplayed by the elegant pedestal wash basin and Cretonne slipcover on the 18th-century chair.

The English firm of Colefax and Fowler created a chintzy country style that has become ubiquitous. George Oakes, head of its design studio, decorated his bathroom in a sleepy green that pervades the bed and bath in his Kent cottage.

SMALL BATHROOMS

Whoever said 'small is beautiful' was obviously not thinking of the bathroom. As a ubiquitious feature of many older houses and apartments, the small bathroom boasts mean proportions that demand ingenuity and economy of design. Every element—the layout and the lighting, the choice of colors and fittings—takes on far greater importance when space is at such a premium.

Fortunately, style is not dependent on scale. Very often the spirit of a room is expressed most powerfully in a single detail such as an antique porcelain soap dish or a one-of-a-kind sink. High Tech provides the model for a small space aesthetic. Its functionalism and simplicity are so supremely practical for cramped city apartments, and offer valuable design lessons for small spaces.

A single pale wash on the walls and windows, ceiling, and even the floor will visually expand an area; combinations of colors, patterns, and surface finishes invariably call attention to the modest dimensions of a room. Similarly, lighting is best kept simple. A single light at the mirror, for instance, should provide illumination adequate for bathing too, but not enough to reveal how small the area is; over-illumination will bring walls closer.

With careful design, every inch of precious space can be used. Medicine cabinets should be recessed

A custom corner sink is sometimes the only way to capitalize on every area of a small bathroom. Here the architect chose a studiously simple look, pared down to essentials.

when possible, and contain a mirror and light. Corner spaces are often wasted, but there are elegant bathtubs, sinks, and toilets designed to take advantage of these areas. Corner tubs are available as small as 36 by 42-inches, as well as toilets that take up as little as 30-inches of floor space, and sinks that project 18-inches or less. Few designs are more space-efficient than those for boats and airplanes, and sinks and toilets can be ordered from such specialist suppliers for the most minute areas.

Still, the tub is normally the largest and therefore the most dominant fixture in a bathroom and when space is limited its color should be chosen to downplay its size—by using a pale shade or one that merges with the surrounding tiles. Sinking the tub in the floor visually diminishes its presence, but the most extreme solution is simply to do away with it altogether and create a completely tiled "wet room" with a floor sloping to a drain.

The quickest, most powerful, and most economical way to increase space and light is by installing mirrors. But as they simply repeat the areas they reflect, mirrors must be positioned with care. In a small bathroom the echoing reflection of a tiny, cluttered area can only serve to make it look smaller. Ideally, mirrors should extend space by reflecting a window view or plants or a treasured photograph.

Good design should outwit spatial limitations, as in this attic conversion in an English farmhouse. The installation of a generous skylight added light and sense of space beneath the eaves without violating the traditional architectural lines of the building.

An area in a cramped basement in Milan was used to the fullest by installing an oval corner shower and corner sink. A single neutral color—in this case powder gray—disguises the limited space.

Windows do furnish and enlarge even the most meager space with precious light and views. Artificial light cannot match natural light for adding subtle moods and variety to any room, while window views increase the perspective of the space.

SMALL
BATHROOMS

Vertical slats of dull-polished aluminum afford a High Tech privacy without further enclosing the small space of this Italian bathroom. Monochromatic colors in the all-smooth, all-hard surfaces appear to enlarge its narrow space.

The encompassing checkerboard tile makes the architectural lines of this tiny English bathroom virtually disappear, creating a dazzling illusion of space. Not for the timid bather, bold colors or patterns can sometimes have the reverse effect than expected.

*T*he bathtub being the largest element in most bathrooms, even a plain shower curtain can diminish the space. Here a folding glass shower screen can be pushed back and is barely noticeable when not in use.

*P*ossibly the ultimate in space-saving bathrooms are those designed to squeeze into awkward areas on planes, boats, or trains where space is severely restricted. This tiny stainless steel sink and toilet designed by John Walmsey for British Rail are virtually indestructible too.

SMALL
BATHROOMS

*D*esigner Steven Holl imagined this bathroom as a Roman atrium in feeling. Extensive use of black Verdi marble veined in white cools down the Fra Angelico red walls. The plaster was applied with a fresco technique using integral color. The porcelain sink, custom-designed, brushed brass towel bars, and sand-blasted glass in the lighting fixtures carry the traditional materials theme throughout the room.

*T*his compact shower-in-the-round from Hastings Tile Il Bagno seems to float in mid-air and is an excellent solution for a limited space. The capsule incorporates recessed shelving area and heated towel bars.

A compact bathroom was created in an unused corner on a second floor landing in this London house. A new, undulating cork wall separates off the area without constricting the hallway.

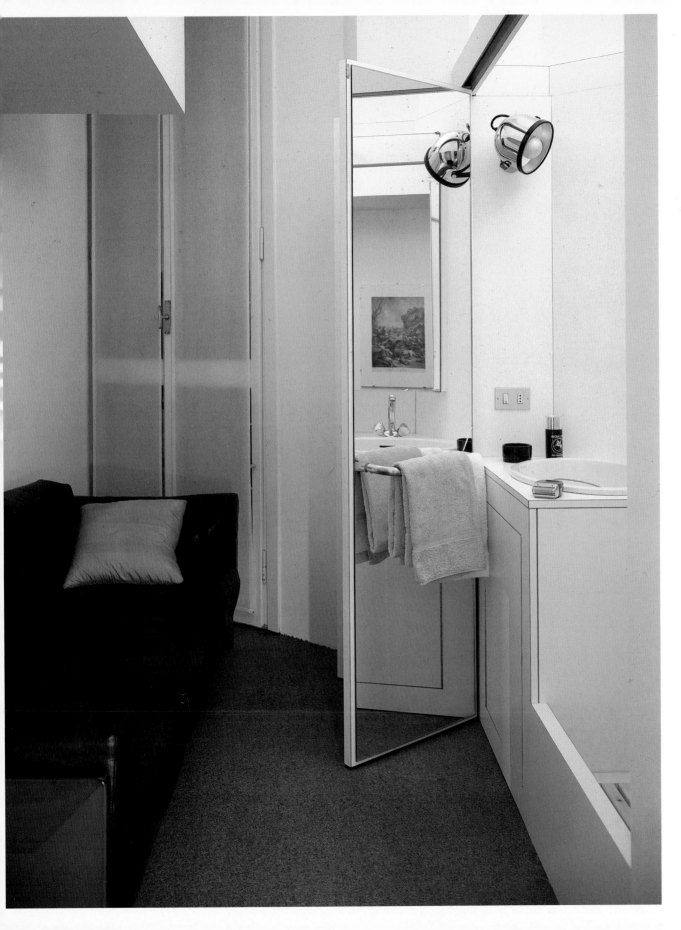

*E*xquisite use of color is the main feature of this guest room bath set into a closet. The neon color accents of lime and electric blue are played against the neutral black leather sofa, white wall, and mirrored door. The sink and shower are neatly set into the wall, to be concealed completely by the folding door.

CHILDREN'S BATHROOMS

In the best of all worlds, children would have their own bathrooms, with smaller sinks, shorter tubs, and lower toilets. The ideal child's bathroom would be safe, self-cleaning, and indestructible. In its absence, designing a bathroom for a child becomes an art in itself.

In the past, liberal use of primary colors and wallpaper featuring cartoon characters was considered the appropriate decoration for a child's room. But today's children are more visually sophisticated, allowing the design a greater freedom.

From a practical point of view, modifying a bathroom for children need not involve major work. Non-slip and waterproof surfaces should be installed on the floor. Specially treated cork is warm, soft, and absorbs sound; linoleum and studded rubber tiles have similar advantages and come in a wider range of colors. Lever-type door handles are easier for small hands to operate than doorknobs, but bathroom doors shouldn't lock from the inside. If adults require privacy, locks should be placed out of a child's reach.

Electricity in the bathroom can present endless hazards. All outlets should be covered with safety plugs when not in use. Light switches should be low enough for children; the best place for the switch is in a lit area outside the bathroom. Also, a night light is important.

The medicine cabinet and supply cupboard for cleaning agents

Designer Alan Tye set a sink and mirror at child's height to make the bathroom less formidable. The single mixer tap is easy for small hands to operate, as is the removeable shower head. Every surface can be washed down when soap suds begin to cling.

and other poisons should be out of reach and securely locked. Sharp metal or glass edges so common on countertops and vanities, should be bypassed in favor of softer materials, softer contours. A sturdy stool set on a non-slip surface will help a child reach the sink and toilet. For younger children, a mirror set at their height will provide great fascination while encouraging good hygiene.

Children often have difficulty regulating water flow and temperature. Thermostatic controls and lever-style faucets that are clearly marked and easy for a child to use will avoid scalding accidents or regular floods.

In a full-size tub, small children will slide around, so a toddler's bathtub and a non-slip rubber mat are very practical. Grab rails around the shower or tub and a hand-held shower will make washing easier and safer.

*E*ach detail in this child's fantasy bath is designed to accomodate a child's growth from age four to nine. High style details evoke a castle atmosphere appealing to children without being coy. Ramparts lead to the bed area over a pneumatic wood drawbridge. The Gothic arched mirror is peaked with an etched coat of arms.

*T*he tub is set in extra wide surrounds of yellow pine that act as a seat for a supervising parent. Tub height is child level for easy access. The designers, Windigo Architects, installed the platform floor a foot above the original (and still existing) floor. When the platform floor is taken up, both sink and tub will be at standard height.

BATHROOMS FOR THE DISABLED

A below–sink lever operates the water in this specially–designed bathroom.

Historically, the bathroom is the most hazardous room in the house: the proximity of water to electricity, and the numerous hard and sharp surfaces combined with wet or slippery conditions, make it a place where the design must consider safety among its priorities. In many respects planning for a disabled user puts all the safety precautions of an ordinary bathroom into the forefront of the design. At the same time, there is a range of products from grab rails to adjustable toilet seats that are sufficiently well-designed to produce an attractive environment that doesn't appear institutional. Standard fixtures that can be used easily are often preferable to a lot of gadgetry. Often the best solutions are given by the user or users themselves. They and their physicians or physical therapists are likely to know the kinds of requirements a design should take into account. Generally, design for the disabled is covered by local codes and these should be allowed for in the planning.

Softer, non-slip materials such as studded rubber tile or cork are a good choice for the flooring. As a general rule, the floor area should be kept clear, uncluttered, and on one level. The total area should be generous in size, with space to allow as much room for movement as possible. Grab rails should be installed around the tub, shower, and toilet, and the entire area should be well-lit, with night lights for the

fixtures. Different colors or textures can be used to define changes of surface clearly. Since the accumulation of condensation makes surfaces more slippery, an efficient ventilation system is recommended.

Electrical installations in the bathroom are covered by strict codes. Outlets and electrical switches should be positioned at a set distance from water sources. Lighting should be properly housed, especially if it is in a damp area.

If the bathroom is to be used by a person in a wheelchair, the entrance should be simple and direct, with no change of level. Inside there must be a clear area of at least 5-feet square to allow for maneuvering. Alexander Kira's in-depth study of bathroom design, *The Bathroom Book* (Viking Press, 1976), recommends that a bathroom for a wheelchair user should be at least 6 or 7-feet by 10-feet. Wheelchair users also need a generous space next to the toilet in which to transfer themselves. Wall-hung toilets can be adjusted to the right height for the wheelchair (about 19 to 21-inches) and generally allow closer access.

Sinks that are wall-hung also allow clearance for a wheelchair. (Hot pipes beneath the sink must be well-insulated to avoid burns.) Plenty of easily reachable storage and counterspace should be at hand to make washing easier, along with a moveable mirror and attached light. The controls on the faucets should

*T*he ideal bathroom for the disabled user should be evenly lit, obstruction–free, with clear access and plenty of supports.

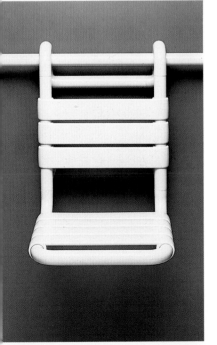

A moving shower seat reduces the risk of accidents and makes washing easier for the elderly, disabled, or invalid.

BATHROOMS FOR THE DISABLED

be easy to operate and reach: hospital style blade hot and cold controls or a single hand lever faucet or special under sink knee-operated lever are the most practical. Better still would be a large push-button or electronic sensor to activate the water flow. Thermostatic water controls are advisable especially if the temperature of the water fluctuates unexpectedly.

TUBS AND SHOWERS

The movements necessary to get in and out of a bathtub have always been problematic for many disabled and elderly people. Even with well-positioned grab bars there is a point when the body is balanced on one foot resting on a wet slippery surface. For the wheelchair user tubs are an even greater obstacle. Recent studies at the University of Wisconsin have come up with designs which can be entered in a sitting position and the tub then rotated or enclosed to be filled with water. Among other recommendations the study also suggested that tubs for the elderly or disabled should be fitted with a cushioned back rest.

Access to showers is not as problematic even for the wheelchair user, as long as the area is wide enough and does not include an entrance curb. The entire area should be lined with a grab rail and include a seat and separate hand shower for washing.

Dansk Pressalit is one of the leading European manufacturers of specialized bathroom fixtures. This wash basin moves up and down for children or wheelchair users, and the single lever tap on the basin facilitates use.

Stepping in and out of the tub is one of the most difficult and hazardous movements in the bathroom for the elderly or disabled. Well-positioned grab rails are almost essential to provide secure support, and some form of intermediary seat, such as on this Universal Rundle bath/shower, will minimize the risk of a fall.

SECOND
BATHROOMS

If the bathroom has historically often been the stepchild of residential design, then the second bathroom has been its neglected orphan. Traditionally set off an entrance hall or guest room, it was comfortless, sparsely furnished, and forgotten except as a repository for ugly or cumbersome odds and ends that the family could not throw away.

Consisting only of a sink and toilet, the traditional half bath was a natural facility for visitors, and architects normally located it with that in mind. In houses it might be placed beneath the staircase in the entrance hall, recalling spacious rooms where visitors waited to be announced. In recent times, architects have tended to drop the half bath in their pursuit of the economies of design and costs, but in truth it more than earns its meager space. A half bathroom, no matter how compact, is a simple means of compensating for lack of space in a main bathroom. Similarly it frees the main bathroom to be more personal, perhaps to become a master bathroom proper.

Square foot for square foot, the installation of a second bathroom is probably the most valuable improvement to the home. Well-designed, it provides all the benefits of a half bathroom, yet needs only marginally more space to include a tub or shower. But the stereotype of the second bathroom is as a smaller, meaner, and consequently less com-

fortable copy of the main washing area. Yet this need hardly be the case. A second bath can give scope for a less traditional concept of bathing by making a sauna or hot tub the focus of the layout. Beyond functioning as an additional facility, it will add a leisure bathing area to the home. Where the main bath may have whirlpool and steam room, for example, the second room could include a sauna with access to a hot tub or exercise area.

When partner to a master bathroom, a second bath can be something of an alter-ego decoratively. If a master bath is designed to assert one personality, the second bath can be a place to indulge a con-

trasting, usually less personal, side, perhaps one more frivolous.

But in many cases the additional bath has a specific purpose, such as being for children or guests, or a location that predetermines its decor and planning, such as being adjacent to a study or studio. Under these circumstances, form most definitely follows function, although of course need not be circumscribed by it.

This second bath was added to a barn conversion in Northamptonshire, England. Wood walls and ceiling were left open and unpainted in keeping with the main part of the house.

*L*avish applications of emerald green brought sophistication to this small bath, even to the green washing machine. Walls and floors are covered with durable rubber studded tiles. The only other color influence is the bold and brilliant hot mustard in the pair of posters.

*T*ucked under the eaves of an older Italian house, this step-down bath is private and cozy. A study in spatial economy, the room is designed to accommodate the needs of guests staying overnight or over the summer.

SECOND
BATHROOMS

On Sutton Place in New York City, this large-dimension treatment of the usually miniscule bath without tub uses Regency red and black, and a startling opaline pink basin.

Charles Jencks calls the half-bath near the entrance to his London house the "Cosmic Loo". The play on words becomes thematic: "cosmos" is stencilled on the ceiling to symbolize the "order of the universe". "Cosmetic" relates to the ritual of putting on one's face in order to face the world. "Cosmopolite", or "over the world", is represented by the frieze of postcards of the family's favorite places around the world.

Toilet and tub were always located in separate rooms before the age of indoor plumbing, and there are those who still insist their combination in one room a less than civilized custom. This small English 'compartment with fixtures' in mahogany and brass is a modern interpretation of the traditional arrangement.

EXERCISE BATHROOMS

Combining exercise and bathing is no modern fad: bathing was part of the gymnastic and exercise routine in ancient Greece. But today, the availability of more compact exercise equipment and home saunas, steam rooms, and whirlpools means that an exercise routine can be more easily integrated into the home, most likely in the bathroom. For many the privacy and convenience of a home area is the only way to keep up an exercise routine. This may be no more than a warm-up and stretching area, or a place for yoga, or it can be a year-round exercise health spa.

Regular exercise can have several related benefits: it improves aerobic health, adds to muscular development, contributes to weight control, and lowers physical stress and tension. The very best forms of exercise produce all these benefits in varying proportions, though some serve to emphasize one more than the others; and the routine and the types of equipment in a home gym should be chosen with personal exercise goals in mind.

With aerobic conditioning, the goal is to improve the cardiovascular system through 20 to 30 minutes of an overall exercise such as swimming or jogging. The extended hard work will increase the heart rate considerably, and maintaining this accelerated rate strengthens the heart muscle.

Muscular strength is increased through exercises in which the muscles work against some resistance; lifting weights is the most obvious example, sit-ups and push-ups the most basic.

Exercise is often made part of a weight control program, most commonly because of the toning effect it has on muscles. This type of exercise can need little more than a mat and routine of coordinated exercises. Relaxation or the reduction of muscular tension is probably the one form of exercise most easily accommodated by any bathroom. A hot bath can achieve this, but of course a whirlpool tub, steam bath, sauna, and hot tub are far more effective and enjoyable.

In contract with the washing areas, an exercise area should have a soft, non-skid floor or be covered with an exercise mat with a slipcover of canvas or other natural fiber. Moderate, uniform lighting is best; room temperature should be adjustable so that it is not too warm and stuffy or puritanically cold. Good ventilation is necessary, both to insure plenty of air circulation and control odors.

Obviously the surroundings for exercise exert a powerful influence on the enjoyment, frequency, and therefore, the results. Perhaps the ultimate in favorable climates is a solarium with an adjoining bath or pool area for exercise and bathing. In the summer, the area can be opened; in winter, it can be enclosed behind sliding glass. Generally, however, views can help diminish the tedium of a repetitious routine . . . as will music or evolving arrangements of favorite momentos, family photographs, and fresh cut flowers.

Even finely honed storage skills can be severely tested by the challenge of exercise equipment. Manufacturers are now responding to this need, and devices such as rowing machines, ski machines, and collapsible cycles can be folded and stored. (Universal and Nautilus types of equipment are stationary; so are treadmills.) Closets will hold portable equipment such as jump ropes, exercise mats, slant boards, and hand weights.

Many doctors feel that a variety of exercises is more beneficial than the same length of time with a single repetitive routine such as jogging or jumping rope. Various types of equipment—rowing machines that give blood pressure readouts, stationary bicycles recording speed and distance, cross-country ski machines, and even stretching machines are far more beneficial when combined with other exercises in a proper routine.

The most advanced weight machines have hydraulic or pneumatic cylinders and cams to provide a balance between pressure and resistance and to reduce the possibility of an accident. The hand weight is highly recommended, not for serious bodybuilding or weight lifting, but very often to improve the efficiency of aerobic exercise and to

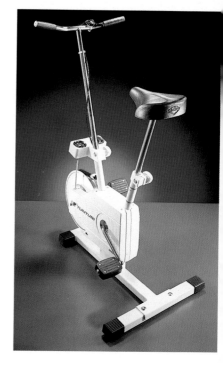

A compact bicycle may be the answer for a smaller exercise bath. Made in Finland by Tunturi, this model is complete with speedometer and odometer.

strengthen different muscle groups.

Some jogging treadmills cost several thousand dollars and can measure speed, distance, and heart rate, but for most people this is an unnecessary extravagance. Ski machines are becoming increasingly popular and are more widely regarded as beneficial because they exercise both the upper and lower extremities. Generally speaking, better quality equipment will last longer, and it will cost more. When a particular kind of equipment is appropriate, it may be better to invest in the more expensive models. In the end, professional advice may be the best investment of all.

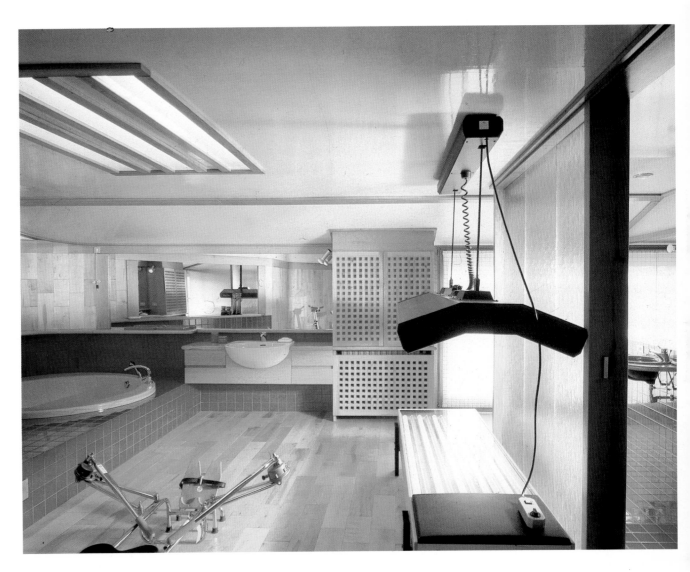

*T*his bath-exercise room in the wine country of Brescia merges the image of majestic, old world spa with new age American exercise mecca. In the money-is-no-object room, cool, high-gloss blonde oak plays off hot, lipstick red sink.

*T*he blonde wood softens the exercise area, and gleaming red tile sparks the wet areas. Beyond the sink are the toilet and sauna. A glazed partition divides the gym and tanning area from the wet area and the private cubicle for commodes.

INDOOR-
OUTDOOR

Bathing *al fresco* is the original way in which man washed or simply soaked. There remains something truly elemental about the experience, so that for many the ultimate bathroom is not one equipped with gadgetry or decorated with luxurious materials, but one that puts the bather outdoors.

Hot tubs have probably done more than anything else to reintroduce indoor-outdoor bathing to western culture. For the Finns or the Japanese it is an ancient and unquestioned tradition against which our customs seem prudish, insensitive, or plain unimaginative. A tranquil view or sunny garden is bound to enhance the benefit of a relaxing soak. Much in the same way, after a swim or a long run, there is nothing quite as invigorating as a shower outdoors in the sun.

In climates that do not facilitate year-round bathing, the bathroom can be installed in a greenhouse extension or solarium, to be opened up in warmer weather. A large skylight or glass-enclosed tub area provides the next best substitute.

In keeping with its spirit, outdoor bathing should generally be kept simple and natural. Natural materials—wood, stone, slate, even beach pebbles—inevitably blend more harmoniously with the surroundings outdoors but are still most effective when used as discreetly as possible. The aim of the indoor-outdoor bathroom, afterall, is to reduce, not establish, boundaries!

Flowers and shrubs can be used to conceal the area or the line of the design, and still further add privacy.

Showers are obviously the easiest of outdoor bathing facilities to install, needing only good water pressure and access to a drain. They make a refreshing end to a day at the beach and with children save a lot of wear and tear on the main bathroom.

Pristine white tiles contrasted with black grouting line this outdoor shower area on a California deck.

A sliding door in a "Miesian" grid provides access to the verdant pool area.

In keeping with the design of the original Mies van der Rohe house, Peter Gluck looked to Japan for inspiration of the bathhouse addition. Between two bedrooms he placed a shower area and a deep, thermostatically controlled soaking tub.

INDOOR-
OUTDOOR

*P*alm fronds from the indoor conservatory adjacent to this magnificent twin shower and bath all but invade the room. Shades of clear gel pull down for privacy on both sides of the tub, while dappled courtyard light is still admitted through a leaded glass window high on the wall.

*R*eminiscent of Arcadia, this private yet completely open bath is ornamented with decorative Greek capitals atop the columns and lush greenery. The sunken bath and shower are shielded from wind and direct sun. Stepping stones (some are shaped like fish) form a grassy walk to the house. Louvered doors from the garden flank the entrance to the bathroom.

Inside, the mirror over the vanity reflects the outer area, further breaking down the indoor-outdoor boundaries.

INDOOR-OUTDOOR

*H*and-glazed tiles underline the geometry yet at the same time relieve its powerful lines with their saturated colors and opalescent sheen.

*A*sked to create a spa addition to a ranch-style Los Angeles house, Mel Bernstein chose to keep the exterior in the spirit of the main house and confine architectural innovations to the interior. The centerpiece of this new 'inner world' of sauna, steam room, and bathing area is the pool set beneath a large skylight. Sliding glass doors open onto a deck area, visually connecting indoor and outdoor areas.

*U*sing the 'divine' proportions of the golden section and the symmetry of the equilateral triangle, Bernstein sought to join spiritual with physical harmony of the spa in a unity of body and spirit.

Left and right of the entrance to the pool are the sauna and steam rooms. Each is windowed, giving a view over the pool to the deck outside.

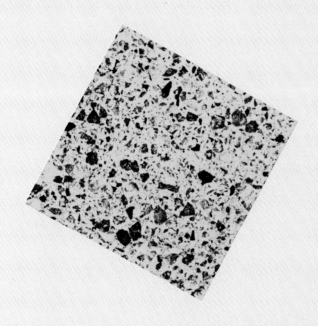

THE
ESSENTIALS

SINKS AND FAUCETS

Nature sculpted the first sink out of rock, creating a place where people could refresh themselves in rain water or the waters from a nearby spring. For centuries a ewer and basin, of silver for the richest, were the principal means of washing. The washstand appeared in the 19th-century. Its various ornamentations were symbols of wealth for the middle classes and paved the way for the modern sink with full plumbing

Most sinks share a curvilinear shape, but there the similarity ends. Natural and synthetic materials, colors from the palest to the most assertive, and dozens of textures and patterns offer enormous variety of choice. By design, installation can glorify or camouflage a sink. In its simplest form, a sink fits into a countertop. Self-rimming sinks have a seal-forming ridge that sits on the counter. Wall-mounted sinks are easier to install and can be positioned at any height. Frequently the most decorative design, the pedestal sink has a central supporting stem that betrays its ancestry in the washstand but also serves to conceal the plumbing. In recent years the pedestal has enjoyed a revival of its popularity, and besides the classic designs, newer streamlined versions have updated its elegance.

SINK MATERIALS

No longer carved from rock, sinks are made from a variety of materials. Ceramic vitreous sinks are the most traditional. They are extremely durable and easy to clean, but they are heavy and do require strong support systems. Modern inset metal sinks often use pressed steel with colorful enamel finishes. Again, they last a long time but are sometimes sensitive to abrasive cleaning agents. High Tech brought to the bathroom the stainless steel sink, which is easy to clean and resistant to heat, chipping, and chemicals.

Modern synthetics such as Corian are expanding the range of shapes, patterns, and possibilities for custom units. One-piece counter-sink units of synthetic are easier to maintain and install, though not quite as rugged.

Poorly designed sinks—those that are too small, too shallow, too low, or with awkward faucets—are the kind of persistent aggravation that can quickly accumulate. In the United States, the largest standard sinks are about 20 by 18-inches (rectangular) to 19 by 17-inches (oval) to a 19-inch diameter (round). According to Alexander Kira in his definitive study of bathroom design, a comfortable working height is 38-inches from the floor.

This modern reproduction of a turn-of-the-century pedestal sink by Sherle Wagner illustrates the timelessness of traditional bathroom design. Sculpted soap holders in a graceful floral design, brass taps, and a Porthault towel complete the effect.

The sinuous curved front of this Dutch pine vanity evokes a warmth, and lightness belies its size. The two graceful ovals of the sinks echo the curvature of the vanity.

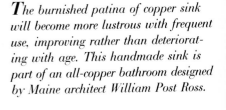

The burnished patina of copper sink will become more lustrous with frequent use, improving rather than deteriorating with age. This handmade sink is part of an all-copper bathroom designed by Maine architect William Post Ross.

This sleek stainless steel recessed sink with its spare single lever faucet is set into the warm-toned maple counter.

A one-legged antique porcelain sink is a handsome addition to this almost unbathlike room. Pictures, burgundy wall color, and carpet provide an unusually rich toned environment.

SINKS AND FAUCETS

A choice of sink should not be made apart from consideration of the style of faucets it requires. For those whose preferences are well developed in this area, the absence of a mixer or single lever faucet will diminish the most glorious marble basin.

Most sinks come with holes already for the faucets (those that don't are generally designed to fit into a countertop and therefore almost any type of faucet can be used with them). The number and distance between the holes dictates the kind of faucet they can take. The best faucets are made from brass and come in a variety of finishes—ranging from chrome or acrylic to silver or gold, and sometimes include a contrasting material such as porcelain or even a semi-precious stone to distinguish the heads.

Most American faucets are mixer types, that is the water comes out of a single spout. The controls, however, follow a variety of forms and can be single lever, center-set (attached to the spout), or spread-fit (with hot and cold controls separate from the spout).

Several types of faucet include thermostatic controls, while one or two designs even feature a moveable spout to facilitate other activities such as hair washing. Automatic faucets operated by an electronic cell to deliver water at a pre-set temperature are in the future for the average bathroom.

Boston designer Janet Allen used hand-painted flowers and apricot-sponged faucets to bring this old marble sink back to life. Fabric ruffles echo the pattern and colors, softening the interior of this three-quarter tiled bathroom.

Colorado designer Yvonne Short custom-made this self-rimming porcelain sink. The crazed, crackled pattern produced in the firing process resembles that of precious glazed pottery. Fat porcelain taps are a modern version of the old fashioned classic.

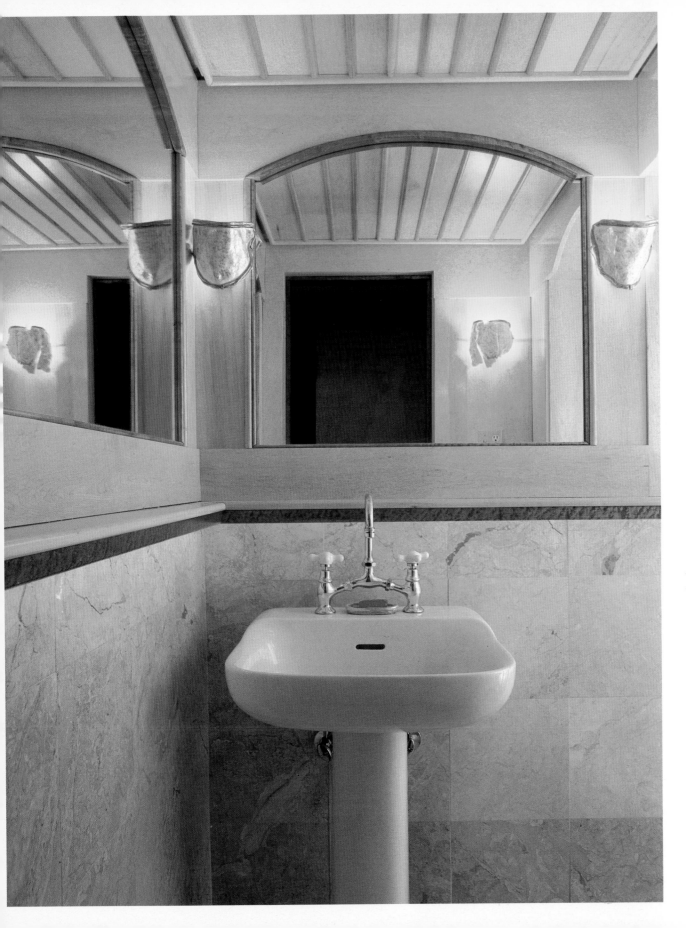

*P*edestal sinks can have an almost sculptural elegance without any cluttering of plumbing or cabinetry. San Francisco-based Osburn Design let this modern version stand alone in a mellow-toned bathroom.

TOILETS AND BIDETS

Like the language that is still used to describe it, the toilet took various imaginative and colorful forms designed to conceal its true purpose before the Victorians developed a modern wash-down closet. (Language or rather slang again misleads us here, for though credited to Thomas Crapper, the invention may belong to the rival London firm of Humpherson.)

While our decoration of the modern toilet is much less exuberant and varied than that of the Victorians (who used floral patterns, bucolic scenes, sometimes even illustrations of political foes), its original shape has remained largely unchanged. Alexander Kira's examination of the minutae of our bathroom habits concluded that not only is its shape uncomfortable and in need of redesign but also that the healthier posture would be a deep squat rather than the more passive sitting position encouraged by most Western toilets.

Vitreous china was used by the Victorians and is still the most popular and widely accepted material for the toilet bowl. Durable, heavy, resistant to stains, chips, and scratches, it is easy to clean and can be manufactured in one hygienic piece. While manufacturers offer toilets in dozens of pastels, some solid colors, and many shades of white, to match their tubs and sinks, toilets do not come in an equal variety of shapes. Units are either two-piece, with a separate tank and bowl, or the more compact one-piece. Both types can be floor or wall-mounted; wall-mounted models tend to appear sleeker but may require special structural work.

Toilets differ most obviously in their systems of flushing. For decades the prevalent design was the wash-down toilet. Now this is being replaced by quieter, more efficient systems, and in some areas the wash-down is actually unacceptable by code. A reverse-trap flushing system is quieter but less preferable to a siphon flush toilet, which is quieter still, less likely to clog, and combats odors more efficiently. Most expense of these is the one-piece, siphon action flush. Water-saving models that use up to a third less water are available for most types of flushing systems.

Without shelf, drawer, or even tooth-brush holder, and with a mirror small enough to reduce vanity to the minimum, this bath in the London flat of Dutch art dealer Hester van Royen is pure Zen. Even the mixer tap on the sink has been eliminated by designer John Pawson.

*O*ne of the earliest extant water closets is in the Turret Room at Osterly Castle in Middlesex, decorated by Robert Adam in 1762. The throne-type treatment of the toilet (completely hidden behind the wood panelling and hinged lid) is a fine example of the euphemistic treatment of the lowly commode.

TOILETS AND BIDETS

In its simplest form the douche dates back to early Rome. But perhaps because of their association with Parisian bordellos early this century, bidets have often been considered slightly naughty. Times have changed since moral crusaders managed to get the Ritz Carlton Hotel in New York to remove their newly installed bidets, although for a nation so hygiene-conscious, bidets remain surprisingly rare.

Like toilets, bidets are made of vitreous china and are generally sold in coordinated designs and colors. Obviously if it is to serve its main purpose, the bidet should be positioned next to the toilet, with enough room for access. Most models are oval in shape and require a straddling position, usually facing the wall, although there are chair-type designs. Simplest is the model that is fitted with faucets and fills up like a basin. More advanced models have mixing valves for water temperature control, and water flushes around the rim. More sophisticated still, and possibly most hygienic, are bidets that incorporate an ascending spray located in the center of the bowl, enabling the user to wash only in clean, running water. Like all plumbing, bidets are governed by local regulations and these should be consulted before any model is chosen.

The elongated toilet and bidet are typical of many of the sleek, streamlined models available. American Standard produces these water-saving units in roguish pale pastels of pink, mauve, and the gray shown here.

*T*he cool stillness of white fixtures often needs special handling. Here the warm wood radiator and window frames and especially the terracotta tiles, which have been hand-enameled in varying shades of gray, enhance the white. The 'decreasing' arrangement of the tiles unifies the toilet and bidet to the area.

*P*ainted wood wainscotting and delicate leaded Tiffany-style stained glass lend a turn of the century feeling to a bath in an otherwise all-white house in Milan. Although both fixtures and fittings are modern, they have a more traditional style.

*B*idet and toilet are given their own private cubicle in this opulent bath lined in Pakistani onyx. Even the recessed towel bar is set in onyx.

SHOWERS AND STEAM BATHS

Ardent shower fans extol its virtues over the bath for convenience, speed, economical water use, and its constant supply of clean water. In addition, they argue that the shower is far more invigorating than the sedentary bath.

The beauty of a shower is its simplicity. But this does not mean it can't be luxurious. While the shower may have been second choice, when there wasn't enough room for a tub, designers are now opening up the traditional shower stall and moving away from its claustrophobic past. By giving the shower an area of its own, multiple shower heads can be installed, together with seating and other bathing conveniences.

Shower and steam room are natural companions, and several manufacturers offer conversion kits with vapor-tight doors and steam generators to adapt existing showers. Combination shower/steam units that drop into position are also on the market.

Shower heads are usually adjustable for the angle of the spray, and in some showers the height of the head can be altered too. More luxurious are the full-length body showers which can a series of jets or angled shower heads; individual controls orchestrate a light or full spray or a pulsating massage. A hand-held shower massage delivers several thousand invigorating pulses per minute. A variation on the shower massage includes an electronic impulse shower that jets hot and cold water alternately to tone the skin and circulation.

STEAM BATHS

Because the damp heat of a steam bath requires only a compact, vapor-tight room with a steam generator that uses very little power, more enclosed shower areas are being converted to accommodate them. Temperatures in the steam room (110° to 130°F) are not as high as those in the sauna, so a greater variety of materials can be used to cover the walls and floors, their ability to withstand the effects of the steam being primary. Flooring should be non-slip, and made of cement or some other textured surface, and be equipped with a drain in the center. Like saunas, the size of a steam bath tends to be limited by the capacity of the heater, and one or two-person steam baths are the most common. The compact steam generator can be positioned several feet away, in an adjoining room or closet.

Japanese porcelain tile lines this shower in designers Bromley-Jacobson's New York loft, creating a single, large wet area that includes seating. One of a pair of master bathrooms, its partner shower offers windows with a view of the Hudson River.

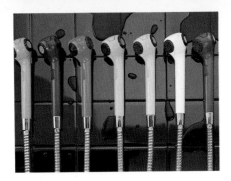

Synthetic materials are injecting vibrant new colors into the once anemic bathroom. These bright Tribel shower heads, by frogdesign in California, are especially practical for small children, enabling adults to wash them in an adult-sized shower area.

Shower areas are especially slippery and hazardous. Hewi's line of colored shower heads, rails, and moveable seats eliminates much of the hopping, even when washing feet.

SHOWERS AND STEAM BATHS

*T*his semi-circular, capsule-like glass block shower bath was designed for a small area by Brian Alfred Murphy, a California architect. Behind the curved wall is the main bath area.

*D*avid Piscuskas for 1100 Architects created a sea-green shower area with imported Venetian glass mosaic that almost shimmers. A deep blue border and tiny centered square define the area, while other textures abound in this master bath, from the marble washing areas to the salmon pigmented plaster.

*T*he waterproof enclosure of a shower stall provides a natural environment in which to create a steam room. Windigo Architects of New Jersey designed this sit-down shower in a renovated 1840s house. The water sprays from three custom vertical rods that run along the length of the shower stall, and can be activated by twisting the rods individually or with the shower faucets.

*A*n antique shower is the major highlight in this couple's bathroom in a Tuscan farmhouse, conjuring up images of Venus ascending from the waters. Nevertheless, there is a High Tech quality about the way the pipes are exposed to become part of the general architecture of the room. The rest of the room also evokes the feeling of another, more gracious time with its high-beamed ceilings, arched shuttered windows, antique porcelain fixtures, and expansive dimensions.

SAUNAS

The Romans were well-acquainted with the health benefits of steam, and built elaborate bathing complexes around the natural hot springs of their empire. The custom of the Turkish bath recognizes the benefits of damp heat and excessive perspiring to rid the body of toxins. Long before the Romans, the North American Indians in their 'sweatlodges' and the Finns in their saunas reclined in dryheat.

Heat, damp or dry, is one of the best body cleansing techniques known, and it also stimulates blood circulation. As with the hot tub and furo, the process of soaping, scrubbing, and rinsing traditionally precedes and follows the sauna or steam bath. But they are two distinct techniques that require different types of equipment.

A Finnish sauna ritual involves perspiration bathing in a 200°F room, cooling off in a cold river or even snow, returning to the sauna, beating the body with fresh birch branches, cooling off again, and after returning to the sauna, a shower. The Finns and many other Northern Europeans enjoy the sauna as a family or communal affair.

In a sauna, the skin is cleansed by intense perspiring, the pores are opened, and the muscles are relaxed. If the heat becomes too intense, water is simply ladled over the rocks. But the cooler the environment, the less perspiration is achieved. Relaxation is as important to the sauna as the alternating exposure to dry heat, cold showers, lakes, or snow. There should be easy access to a place to lie quietly or read before starting the cycle once again.

In Finland, entire cabins are given over to the sauna. They will include the sauna room and a communal room for relaxation after the exposure to heat. Ideally, they are set on the side of a lake or river for cooling plunges. But a proper sauna needs only to have an area sufficient for the bathers to recline in.

The construction of a sauna is basic and straightforward. A small room lined with wood and tight fitting door, double-glazed window, and sauna heater are the necessities. The choice of wood is especially important, not simply for its appearance and fragrance, but to enable the bather to recline or sit comfortably when surface temperatures are high. Finnish raw red pine, redwood, cedar, and aspen are among the most popular choices. A sauna should be further insulated with fiberglass.

Of the kits that are available, some are no larger than closet-size. Rarely is a sauna larger than 12 feet wide for efficient heat circulation. When available space does not determine the sauna's size, it can be settled by the number of people who will use it. A good yardstick is 2 feet of bench space per bather, while 5 feet by 7 feet is the minimum space required for a person lying down.

The 2,000-year-old sauna ritual is spectacularly updated in this Milanese bath where the spartan and the sybaritic are successfully combined. The multiple arched windows of the late Renaissance townhouse frame the exercise area, and the sauna is tucked away near the washing area.

A proper Finnish sauna is not complete without a bracing dip in a chilly lake or river, or a roll in the snow. This example on the shores of a lake in Finland provides a tranquil setting for invigorating exercise. Birch branches are available for the dedicated to beat themselves until they tingle before the icy plunge.

*T*his Finnish sauna is shown in its natural state, bathed in golden light. In the intense heat of a sauna, only wood is safe to touch, and even nails and screws must be sunk to avoid skin contact. Water is ladeled over hot rocks to produce steam when the dry heat passes the point of endurance.

BATHTUBS

As the bed is to the bedroom, the tub is the chief feature of the bathroom. Almost inevitably it determines how the rest of the room will look. Yet until recently, the modern tub was little more than a basin of ample proportions—inelegant, uncomfortable, often too short and slippery. In the past ten years, however, bathtub design has changed more than in the previous hundred years, when the cast iron tub was first standardized.

Even as recently as seventy years ago, only the well-to-do had private baths. These status symbols were frequently outfitted in grand style, and for sheer opulence very few modern fixtures can match a restored antique tub. In most cases, these generous tubs are cast iron covered with a hard, vitreous coating called porcelain enamel. Unfortunately this brittle finish scratches and chips easily. (Stains left by iron deposits and fluoridated water can generally be removed by bleach.)

Antique tubs are cumbersome to move yet surprisingly delicate; the claw feet are particularly fragile. Rarer and more luxurious still are copper tubs, porcelain baths, and regal European marble ovals for bathing. An expert can predict whether a chipped, stained tub may be successfully restored.

An easily overlooked consideration before installing an antique tub is its hardware. European fau-

A massive ball-footed oval tub forms the centerpiece of this French bathroom. Neo-Egyptian and Art Nouveau motifs are repeated throughout the apartment.

cets and those produced before standardization may be incompatible with contemporary American plumbing, so that replacing an item as seemingly insignificant as a missing washer can be as expensive as the tub itself.

MODERN TUBS

Until recently most bathtubs were made of pressed steel with a vitreous enamel coating which was lighter, cheaper, and more durable than cast iron. Acrylic and reinforced fiberglass have been added as materials, and because of their molding qualities they have introduced a welcome range of shapes and contours to the bathtub. At the same time, these synthetic bathtubs are available in greater variety of colors and patterns and can be fairly simply customized. Plastic tubs are available in different thicknesses but it is advisable to choose the heaviest gauge, particularly for larger tubs. One final point: the rich, seductive finish of fiberglass bathtubs is sensitive to scratching and with acrylic can sometimes dull with age.

Genuine old hardware can be difficult to install in existing fixtures but it does provide an authentic finishing touch. This English brass and porcelain hand shower is as ornate and elaborate as an early telephone, a celebration of form and function.

Copper tubs are exquisite but rare relics of 19th century bathroom design. Once a poor relation of the luxury porcelain tub, this French example has lines which betray its close kinship with the portable hip bath.

Black vertical strips of marble define the area around this spacious roll-top tub in a London flat. The tub dates from the 1920s.

BATHTUBS

The whirlpool may be the bath of the future. Essentially a bathtub with an electric pump that creates a swirling motion in hot water, a whirlpool (sometimes called a jacuzzi) brings the benefits of hydrotherapy to the residential bathroom. Immersion in water a few degrees hotter than normal body temperature for 15 to 20 minutes reduces stress. It also lowers blood pressure, soothes muscle tension, opens pores, and improves circulation. So popular is the whirlpcol that more and more architects consider it a standard feature in a new house.

In a whirlpool, water drawn from the bath is mixed with air and then pumped back in an aerated stream through nozzles set around the inside of the bath. On nearly every model the action can be controlled by one or more air valves.

Any model larger than a one-person tub will almost certainly need a one horsepower motor. But the motor will produce a different action depending on the model. Some tubs use as many as six jets to produce high pressure streams; others use fewer jets to produce an overall swirling motion.

Whirlpools are manufactured in the same materials as tubs. Most are fiberglass, but cast iron and even marble and onyx are available. Several manufacturers offer custom colors and will accomodate different design specifications.

Any structurally sound bathroom with good plumbing can take a whirlpool tub. Extra water pressure is not necessary because jets recycle the water, but with larger tubs, the pressure should be sufficient to fill the tub before the water cools. Whirlpool tubs require professional installation, partly to insure that the tub is adequately supported.

Perhaps the most extravagant application of technology to the bathtub is the 'bathing environment'. These whirlpool systems feature varying combinations of stereo, telephone communications systems, water temperature controls, sunlamps, saunas, steam rooms, remote control of audio/video and other appliances throughout the house, facial misters, pillow massage headrests, and even the mundane bath and shower.

A generous double whirlpool seems carved from Italian granite in this dramatic master bath on Manhattan's Upper East Side, designed by Shelton Mindel Associates. The rest of the apartment is sunny and bright, but the bed and bath are deliberately more serene. Sandblasted doors screen the toilet area from the vanity.

A freestanding standard tub is the focal point of this bath in a stone cottage in the Napa Valley of California. The modest white enameled tile of the tub surround blends well with the thick wells of smooth stone. Arched windows fill the room with sunlight.

This all-marble Italian bath takes a minimalist approach that is Egyptian in feeling. The elegant tub is framed in contrasting marble that is also used for the floor. The blue glass soap dish is the only personal touch in this supremely cool and uncluttered bath.

BATHTUBS

Although mass-produced baths are available in circular, square, even cloverleaf shapes that accommodate four and six adults, design constraints or simply personal taste can dictate the form of a custom tub. Several manufacturers will supply special colors, shapes, designs or materials, but an alternative is a site-specific design. These tubs can be created to fit an unusual space or tiled to match a color scheme, effectively becoming part of the architecture. They may be sunken and treated in the same material as the walls or floor, thereby disappearing as a focal point, or for the opposite effect, elevated and approached by steps.

Virtually any waterproof material that is durable enough to withstand regular repetitive changes of wet and dry such as marble, ceramic tile, mosaic, glass block, granite, sealed concrete, metal sheeting, even wood, is appropriate. But for all the possibilities it opens up, a custom tub must be designed and installed by an expert and conform to local plumbing and electrical regulations. Faulty or amateur work could result in damage not only to the bathroom but to the structure of the entire house.

Los Angeles architect Chris Dawson opened up several rooms to create this large master bath. Surrounded by separate steambath, shower, toilet, dressing, and exercise areas, the custom-built, tiled jacuzzi sits beneath a wide skylight.

Fixtures are treated as sculpture in the mode of Marcel Duchamp in this bathroom in a single family home in Venice, California. The site-specific tub becomes a sculptural extension of walls and floor. Although the effect is dramatic, it is also low-budget, as all materials are modest in nature. Architect Fred Fisher used two-inch granite tone ceramic mosaic tile throughout.

The "Dome of Water" jacuzzi by Charles Jencks was inspired by baroque cathedral domes but used conversely for an upside down effect. Overhead is a representation of the earth. Piers Gough designed the inverted room and Simon Sturgis arranged the oval, complete with illusionistic ribs and coffers that curve toward a central lantern. In place of the four evangelists are four glass lights representing the seasons.

HOT TUBS

The American hot tub is descended from the ancient Japanese *furo*, the free-standing wooden communal soaking tub. Like the Scandinavians and some other older cultures, the Japanese conceive of bathing as a social activity, one to be shared by family and friends.

A furo is a tub for soaking, not for washing, which precedes the furo. In typical combination of practicality and philosophy, the furo conserves precious water in Japan and is a therapeutic activity. Customarily the furo is filled to its brim, so that with immersion water spills over and runs into a drain set under a slatted wood floor. Water is not drained but reheated.

Popularized during the 1960s, the American hot tub is also meant for leisurely soaks. Normally it is placed outdoors, where perhaps a sun-filled lake view or garden surrounding is most conducive to relaxation. The tub is partially embedded in the ground for support as full, with two or three occupants, it can weigh three tons.

The water temperature in a hot tub is kept at about 105°F (slightly lower for children) by an oil, gas, or electric heating system. The same water can be recirculated through a pump and filter for up to 3 or 4 months before it needs to be changed. (A tub can be refilled with an ordinary garden hose.) A close-fitting cover keeps the water clean and conserves energy when the tub is not in use.

Vertical grain redwood is the most popular material for tubs, although oak and cedar can sometimes equal it for durability. Teak is unequalled for its resistance to decay and durability, and, unfortunately, for its price.

An increasing number of tubs are molded from fiberglass with an acrylic or gelcoat lining into square, octagonal, or any shape and color desired. Like wooden tubs, they are generally about 4-feet deep and anywhere from 3½ to 12-feet across. Also like hot tubs, installation should be considered into their price and nearly all fiberglass tubs (sometimes called spas) must be installed below ground for support. Spas can also be made from cement, like swimming pools. Both fiberglass and concrete spas require less maintenance that wooden tubs. But the brilliant colors of their acrylic or gelcoat finishes can fade in the sun.

Beyond a basic pump, filtration and heating system, some tubs also add a blower and several jets which increase water movement to produce something closer to the effect of a whirlpool tub. Still more advanced units include timers and automatic cleaning systems.

A hot tub has been set into the floor in this modern porch extension built onto a Connecticut house. The sloping glass ceiling has wood-slatted blinds to let in a dappled light. The extensive use of wood provides a rustic warmth to the modern approach. The result is a feeling of privacy without being closed in.

Hot tub covers are necessary for keeping water clean, reducing heat loss, and as a safety measure. This rolltop cover, made by California Cooperage, is as handsome as the rest of the tub. It is made of wood slats fastened to an insulating foam base, and is light enough to be handled by one person.

*T*he spectacular view of San Diego's Mission Bay from this rooftop made it an inspired site for an "entertainment center." The multi-level area includes a cooking pit, wet bar, greenhouse, and shower in addition to a dining area and the hot tub. Architect Rob Wellington-Quigley has installed a canvas shade on top of the crow's nest for protection from the sun.

HOT TUBS

*T*his Japanese-style bath house in Marin County is an addition to the master bedroom suite. Designed by architect Ted Brown, it is constructed entirely of cedar so that all surfaces can be hosed down. A solar panel on the roof heats the teakwood hot tub. The shower cylinder is of transparent acrylic. Translucent shoji screens diffuse the California sunlight, while glass garden doors open the room to the secluded garden.

Designer Susanne Shaw converted the sun porch of a formal and rather dark old Washington, D.C. home into an indoor-outdoor exercise pool complete with whirlpool and hot tub. To keep *the bathing areas separate, she employed tongue-in-groove wood screens behind which the hot tub is set, along with a small toilet and dressing area. The architect is James Ritter of Alexandria.*

DESIGN DETAILS

LIGHTING

Shafts of country light bathe this attic bed-and-bath with pale sunlight. The generous skylight becomes the main feature of the room, unifying the bed and bath areas of this cozy room into one.

There are few more complex and subtle aspects of design than lighting. Not only does it have an important functional role, but also it is probably the single most influential factor in determining the mood and atmosphere of a room, and therefore in influencing the mood of its occupants. No matter how well-planned or beautiful a room may be, under inadequate or inappropriate lighting its qualities will be disguised or diminished.

Perhaps in no other room in the house has lighting been more clumsily handled than in the bathroom. Although this is a highly intimate room where we start and finish the day, little thought is usually given to using the lighting to create a sympathetic atmosphere.

Few bathrooms enjoy a great deal of natural light and this perhaps as much as the traditional use of harder surfaces and cooler colors has contributed to the sterile atmosphere of the bathroom. Natural light brings a life—as it changes through the day, weather conditions, and season— and a warmth to a room that artificial light can only aspire to reproduce. Put a bathroom in a room with plenty of windows and it is more likely to become a place for lingering and relaxing. Although natural light cannot serve for shaving or applying makeup, it should be taken advantage of, as far as privacy allows. Windows should be left clear or covered with translucent material—frosted or stained

The alternate pattern of clear and translucent glass block bathes this room in an aqueous natural light and yet maintains its privacy.

glass, shoji screens or half blinds— that still admits as much outside light as possible.

Aside from mood, the dimensions of the room, its color scheme, and even its location should be considered in selecting lighting. Bright, even lighting is not necessarily 'good' lighting, especially in a smaller space. Generally, it makes a room look smaller, less interesting, and with so many hard, shiny surfaces it will actually be tiring to look at. Recessed ceiling lights can very often make a low-ceiling room seem higher and shadows created by a single, concentrated light source will actually disguise the mean proportions of a small room.

Anyone who has stepped from the muted, soft light of a bedroom into the startling glare of an overlit, white tiled bathroom will confirm that the lighting in a bathroom should be designed with some thought to its location. Bathrooms should be well-lit in the interests of safety but those that are likely to be visited in the night should strike a gentler compromise.

Like the shapes of things around us, colors change according to the light they are seen in. (In a purely scientific sense, color is light.) In the bright, hard light of a summer's day, for example, only the strongest colors stand out, whereas in the more muted light of an overcast day softer colors, and a greater range of tones are visible. In the same way, the colors (and shapes) in a

Rice paper shades cover the floor-to-ceiling windows of this 18th-century Paris apartment, creating exquisitely luminous, diffuse light. The elegant marble fireplace, salvage shop basin, and old dentist's trolley contribute an eclectic mood.

LIGHTING

Olympic torch sconces illuminate the walls of this couple's minimalist bath. The gleaming all-white tile treatment of the surfaces lightens it considerably, exposing a room where everything serenely rests against a wall. The paired tubs are set head-to-foot to keep the area as open as possible.

bathroom will change both according to the quality of the lighting—direct or indirect, soft or bright—and its color. Of the three major types of residential lighting, tungsten lighting (sometimes called incandescent) gives the warmest colored light—noticeably yellowish and closer in color to man's original 'organic' light source, fire, and its variations in candle, gaslight, and oil lamp.

Fluorescent lighting can approximate closest to the cool, bluish gray hues of muted daylight, although there are several dozen colors of 'white' fluorescents to choose from. Added to its lower energy consumption, longer life, and greater light output this has made fluorescent lighting the choice for many bathrooms. Its diffuse quality reduces eye strain and many of its early problems have been overcome. But many people still find it harsh and relentless and poor usage of fluorescents has certainly contributed to the inhuman, morgue-like atmosphere of many bathrooms.

The latest lighting to appear for the home is the tungsten halogen light (also known as quartz or quartz iodine). It lasts seven times longer than the average tungsten bulb, consumes half the power, is a tenth of the size, and gives out a strong, white, 'high noon' type of light without the yellowish glare of tungsten or the anemic qualities of many fluorescents. More and more fixtures are being designed for tung-

sten halogen, whose main drawbacks appear to be the intense heat it gives off, the fragile nature of the bulb, and its much greater expense.

With some 2,500 bulbs of these three types, in various shapes, sizes, colors, and styles, the choice can be bewildering. A simple way to judge the quality and color of any bulb in the store is to observe how one's hand looks under it. Skin is a sensitive and, for the bathroom, a highly important measure of the light.

To illuminate this completely black and white Los Angeles bathroom, David James used a wall-mounted Italian halogen lamp from Artemide. Highly adjustable, here it lights the slightly skewed mirror and Kroin sink and fittings.

As if to underline the spectacular green-veined marble that covers every surface of this bath, the porthole window has been widely beveled, creating the feeling that the room was carved out of solid stone. Rows of theater lights illuminate the recessed sink area.

LIGHTING

TASK LIGHTING

In nearly every bathroom some form of task lighting is positioned near the mirror over the sink or as part of the complete vanity washing area. Many bathroom mirror units and medicine cabinets contain built-in lighting. But often additional lighting is necessary for shaving, applying makeup, and other meticulous tasks. Task lighting should be positioned above or equally on both sides of the mirror, shining onto the face, not the mirror. Fluorescent light, diffused by a translucent glass or plastic screen, is the most common choice for its even, 'white' light. Several low-wattage tungsten bulbs are frequently mounted in strips around a mirror to achieve a similar, even light, and in this case the total wattage should not exceed about 120-180. (Fluorescent lighting, with its greater output, need only total 40-60 watts around a mirror.)

Lighting is less critical in other areas of the bathroom generally and its design can focus more on decorative effects and less on its purely practical qualities. In shower or steam bath areas where there is high humidity a vapor-proof fixture should be installed.

A common mistake in choosing lighting is to concentrate on the fixture without considering the kind of bulb it takes. But whether for task or ambient lighting, the aesthetics of the unit and the color and quality of the light it gives should not be separated.

AMBIENT LIGHTING

With careful design, the ambient light in a bathroom can become the dominant light for most occasions. A dimmer switch will give a variable range of illumination and these are now available for certain fluorescent bulbs. But in a larger room, with several areas of different activities, lighting can be used more individually as each area demands. Light bounced off the ceiling from wall sconces, for example, will create a gentler, more diffuse effect than, say the areas of intense dark and light thrown by a series of spotlights on a ceiling. With less demand for color fidelity, warmer-colored, more flattering lighting can be installed, perhaps to complement a cooler color scheme or to soften the hard surfaces of the bathroom.

Mixing tungsten and fluorescent light in a room often combines the best of both worlds. To avoid them fighting with each other a warm white (soft white) fluorescent bulb should be used.

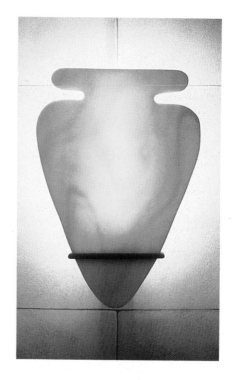

This imaginative urn sconce with streamlined Grecian features by New York designer Jerry Van Deelen sheds a moody diffuse light. Van Deelen used Corian in sheets thin enough to resemble alabaster.

Good lighting design depends less on an understanding of physics and more on defining the tasks it must perform and analyzing the bulbs and the fixtures suitable to meet these needs. The advice of a qualified lighting designer or a knowledgeable lighting store can only help in determining the optimum lighting configuration for a room.

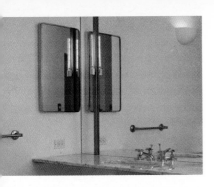

Kevin Walz used halogen lighting in a candle-like tube to illuminate the washing area in this New York bathroom. Another sconce throws a softer, atmospheric light up to be indirectly reflected from the ceiling.

In a bathroom high enough for privacy, the natural light of a cityscape can be freely admitted. This window looks out onto Manhattan towers and water tanks, and is simply framed by a marble counter that runs smoothly from wall to wall.

Scalloped glass sconces are used to throw a gentle light on this Victorian-style sink in the corner of a bedroom. The floral sprigged wallpaper and ornate mirror frame enhance the nostalgic mood.

WALLS

The treatment of the walls, the largest single area, inevitably has a presiding influence over the design of the rest of the room. Even in older buildings, bathroom walls generally have few architectural details of interest—wall and window mouldings may run throughout the house but be absent from this room of 'pure function'. As in other aspects of bathroom design, then, the design must work to introduce interest or decorative qualities without compromising its functional responsibilities.

For wall materials these responsibilities are simple: they should be impervious to water and easy to clean. For many years ceramic tile has fulfilled these criteria with such economy and durability that few other options are ever considered, although modern standardized versions can rarely match Victorian or Art Nouveau tiles for pure decorative qualities.

Waterproof wallpaper generally has a plastic finish that is water-resistant and can be used on any wall that is not regularly soaked such as a shower area. The range of wallpaper colors, patterns, and stripes even extends to likeable imitations of more luxurious materials such as marble, or painstaking paint effects like sponging. Where different rooms such as bed and bath, or bed and master bath are contiguous or even combined wallpaper, like paint, will underplay the transition in a harmonious fashion. Similarly wallpaper can inject several colors and variations in scale and pattern that are virtually impossible with any other wall treatment.

Paint remains by far the most economical wallcovering in every respect. In the damp environment of a bathroom only oil-based paints should be used. With the revival of the traditional skills of sponging (applying colors with a natural sea sponge), marbling, ragging, or stencilling, for example, paint has taken on a new vigor as a decorative finish. A stencilled border not only adds decorative interest to a plain wall but can also serve to alter the proportions of a room.

Ceramic tile epitomizes the qualities of a bathroom wall surface—it is extremely durable, water-resistant, and easy to maintain. Wall tile is thinner and less robust than floor-grade tile but is available in a far greater range of colors and shapes. In many cases, especially in small bathrooms, a matching wall tile or the same floor tile is used over the floors, walls, and even the ceiling, to expand the area and create a single 'wet' room. Several varieties of hand-made tile can be found which often come in more unusual and intense colors that lack the uniformity which can become tiring in a tiled area. Imported glass mosaic tiles also offer a variety and intensity in their colors that mass-produced ceramic tiles often lack.

Stencilling, a traditional American art form, is happily undergoing a revival. Borders like this of delicious pastel peaches, limes, and cherries add unique detailing to a plain wall, and can be used equally to highlight or disguise architectural features.

This spectacular trompe l'oeil wall, by Trompe Ploy of New York, adds a Spanish-American touch to this otherwise plain sink area.

Trompe l'oeil *is an inexpensive and glamorous way to give a distinctive treatment to a bathroom wall. Here designer Carrie Neighlor-Leyland painted a wandering frieze of chintzy flowers and combined it with shirred chintz to add a sumptuous atmosphere.*

WALLS

Marble is perhaps the most traditional luxurious finish for a bathroom. Its rich, almost aqueous veining and colors have made it the classic choice in sumptuous bathrooms for centuries. Being a natural material, marble is variable in colors, patterning, and quality. Some have very rich patterns and a surprising range of colors in their overall cream, pink, green, or blue-black hues, and these are often the most difficult to match and install. Others have a more uniform appearance.

Laminates are still laboring under the unattractive image of an imitation wood-grain surface material. But modern laminates are available in dozens of colors and patterns that are more natural to the medium. Solicor and Colorcore are probably the most celebrated recent innovations—a series of vibrant, solid colors that are pigmented throughout the material so that the laminate does not show a black line when cut and can be shaped or carved to fit an area. Impervious to stains and water, easy to clean, and highly durable, Corian is similar to a laminate and like some recent laminates, it can be cut and shaped like wood. Again, like laminates, it is used in varying thicknesses or grades.

Chintz wallpaper and matching sweep of floor-to-ceiling drapery create a more domesticated splendor than stone or tile. Water-resistant wallpaper is generally less expensive than tile and easier to replace.

The shimmering greens of this London bath create a submarine effect. Much of its luminous quality results from the use of glass wall panels, which have a milky depth of color.

Cork is a versatile wall or flooring choice with the added benefits of being softer, and good insulation. When used in wet areas, it must be sealed.

*T*he most lavish wall treatment in a bath is a semi-precious stone such as marble, alabaster, or as in this case, Pakistani onyx. The opulence of times past is treated in a nearly austere modern fashion, swept clean of all unnecessary adornment.

WALLS

This unusual alternative to the "same old" approach to tile illustrates how imaginative and decorative tile can be. Executed by California artist Peter Shire for his own Memphis-style bath, the tiles are set-in whimsically akimbo.

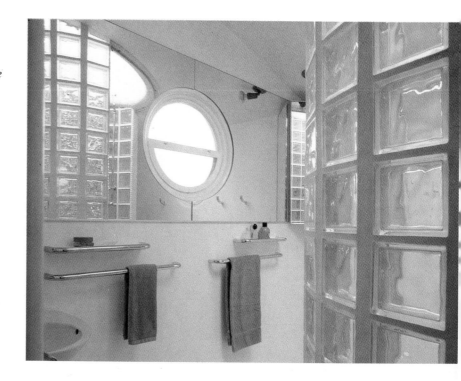

Circular shapes echo in the washing area of this minimalist bed and bath designed by architect Brian Alfred Murphy. The semi-circular glass block wall separates the formal shower bath from the sink and toilet; the symmetrical towel bars sit under a porthole window and baffled skylights.

The exterior of the building is consistent with the interior walls, featuring the same block patterning of different colors and textures. Architect Fred Fisher was trying to give the building the feeling of an archaeological discovery in the mixture of materials.

FLOORS

Flooring materials can be divided into three categories: hard (stone, concrete, wood, or tile), semi-hard (rubber and cork tiles or linoleum), and soft (carpeting). At least some flooring in nearly every bathroom is water-resistant, either hard or semi-hard, and this same material is often extended throughout the entire room.

HARD FLOORS

Ceramic or smaller mosaic tile is the most common bathroom floor, because of its almost indefinite life and ease of maintenance as much for its resistance to water. Tiles for the floor are heavier than wall tiles and can be glazed with a matte or textured finish, or left unglazed with a natural or textured surface. Unglazed tiles tend to be more hardwearing if only because the color runs through the tile, but come in a very limited range of natural colors.

Although one of the more economic forms of floor covering, especially to install, ceramic tile can be designed to achieve more luxurious effects by, for example, combining several colors or introducing contrasting colors into a single background color. Colored grouting will enliven a single plain color, although some find the geometric pattern it highlights overimposing.

Mosaic can be small ceramic (glazed or unglazed), glass, or marble tiles about 1-inch square. Gen-

erally sold in flexible sheets, they can more easily follow the contours of a curved wall or floor than larger tiles. Glass and marble mosaics produce a rich, Mediterranean effect, because of a greater range and depth of colors.

Various types of stone are alternatives to ceramic tile, particularly where a more natural look is desired. Like tile, stone is extremely durable, water-resistant, and easy to clean. Generally not as easy to cut or to install around the awk-

ward shapes in a bathroom as ceramic tile, their true cost should include cutting and installation. Granite and slate are frequently being introduced into the bathroom. Both are non-porous, relatively inexpensive, and come in a variety of finishes that render them more slip-resistant. Slate's muted, darker natural tones make it an ideal choice for an indoor-outdoor area, although it readily shows up water, talcum powder, and most other common spills that a light-toned floor con-

ceals. Granite comes in a far wider range of colors and patterns that runs from pinks and greens to a crisp, speckled black and white.

Terrazzo is a composite of marble chips set in concrete or a softer synthetic resin. Like slate or granite it is sold in tiles and is extremely durable, but its chief attraction is in its greater range of colors. Besides various marble hues terrazzo now comes in lively pinks, greens, blues, and other colors that are favored by both architects and designers.

The hills of the French countryside are framed in this castle bath to raise serenity to new heights. Despite this modern addition, the ancient interior has been left almost uncompromised. One wall is rugged stone and the original smooth floor is a natural finish for a bathroom.

The shower area of this bath continues the two kinds of tile used throughout an adjoining gym area. Pink accents the gray here but in other areas predominates, thereby unifying the walls. In the generous shower area a seat and detachable shower head allows for leisurely washing.

Designed by Pam Scurry, this greenhouse bath has been constructed between a penthouse and an adjoining terrace on Fifth Avenue in New York City. The huge tub is set, mid-room—and virtually mid-Manhattan skyline—in cool white marble. A highly functional unglazed white mosaic floor from Mid-State Tile is given a pastoral freshness by the soft, floral patterned interior wall.

FLOORS

That ubiquitous floor covering—linoleum tile—becomes a visually exciting abstract design under the aegis of New York designer Scott Marks. He breaks up predictable patterns, using and mixing colors dramatically, and throws miniscule variations into his geometry.

Because marble can scratch, chip, or stain (especially the paler colors), it is not often used for floors. A dull or matte finished stone should be selected for a floor as it is less likely to betray minor damage. Glossy, polished marble should be saved for walls or surfaces that are not heavily used. Marble is sold in blocks, tiles, or pre-cut shapes, but whenever possible it should be selected personally for the best results.

Now available are several new synthetic stones that combine the beauty and resilience of natural materials without some of their disadvantages. Neoparium and Quarella more or less reproduce the appearance of marble but are more uniform in color, resistant to abrasion and chemicals, and easier to cut and shape. Zeta Marble is a mix of marble and onyx that produces luxurious-looking but highly practical tiles.

Wood is generally used only in indoor-outdoor bathrooms or outdoor shower or tub areas. Despite its qualities as an economical and attractive material, even thoroughly sealed wood is susceptible to water or chemical damage over time. In outdoor areas where a weathered finish can be desirable, this does not diminish its advantages as a relatively hard-wearing floor.

SEMI-HARD AND SOFT FLOORS

Linoleum and rubber tiles are two very different materials that share many of the same advantages. Both are impervious to water, easy to install and maintain, fairly hard-wearing, and quite soft underfoot. Linoleum, like rubber, comes as tile or sheet but is manufactured in an enormous range of colors and patterns which can be varied further by skilled cutting and laying. Rubber tile was originally used in commercial and industrial situations. Its original, drab colors have been joined by bold, vibrant colors in ribbed and studded patterns.

Cork tile is principally valued for being non-slippery, relatively soft, and excellent sound and heat insulation. Once sealed it will not absorb water, although persistent or prolonged wetting can lead to damage. Although some colors have been introduced, most cork is confined to shades of brown.

There are few more comfortable floor coverings than carpet. Soft and warm underfoot, non-slip, and available in countless colors and patterns, carpeting is nevertheless a difficult choice for the bathroom. Even synthetic fiber carpets will absorb and hold moisture for some time, and natural fiber carpets will quickly begin to rot under repeated soakings. Both also need regular cleaning and washing. From a purely practical point of view, a very durable, rather unglamorous industrial synthetic carpet is the best choice if the bathroom must be carpeted. At the same time, however, there is no reason why carpet cannot be used in combination with a more water-resistant material such as stone or tile.

Contrasting areas of gray and black Japanese tile were used by California designer Chris Dawson in this remodelled master bath. Having joined two smaller rooms, he used this economical color scheme to unify and at the same time separate the different areas in the larger space.

Not for the timid is this Memphis bed and bath. Amoeba-like patterns are set like puzzle pieces in the checkerboard floor, an aqueous touch. Furniture, walls and other surfaces are treated with a similar exuberance and wit.

New York artist Michael Thornton-Smith specializes in trompe l'oeil *and* faux marbre *effects that can transform mundane materials or a dull space. Here painted wood takes on the appearance of a rich marble tiled floor.*

Small spaces generally benefit from a simple, uniform treatment. Here, using a sophisticated gray slate tile, boundaries seem to disappear over the semi-circular steps and up the wall to the tub, maximizing the cramped space.

Marbelized terra cotta lavishly dresses up this otherwise sedate Italian bathroom, establishing a decorative scheme against which all other elements can play. The elaborate border befits the ornate detailing in the 18th–century lakeside villa.

STORAGE

Few are the bathrooms with too much storage. Some might argue that the ability to successfully organize bathroom storage is a rare talent, but in fact the challenge is met with reckoning and a little ingenuity. A realistic evaluation of storage requirements is the first step. For example, the spacious bathroom shared by a fastidious couple can support a meticulous arrangement of everything from towels to toothbrushes. The average family bathroom, however, will always look like the wake of a hurricane if it's lacking separate storage for each person, deep shelves for clean towels, and huge hampers for laundry.

Second only to those of the kitchen, the storage demands of the bathroom seem to become greater and more varied each year. No longer are the ubiquitous medicine cabinet and double-door plywood vanity considered the best way to store bathroom supplies. Beautiful, luxurious bath towels deserve to be seen, and can be stacked on airy, glass shelves. Cleaning agents aren't pretty, but are dangerous; they should be assigned to concealed storage, and locked up if children use the bathroom. Bathing sponges and brushes are best on tub or shower caddies, together with shampoos and loofahs. The blow dryer, curling iron, heated rollers, electric shaver, and other appliances are convenient near a mirror, but their cords are hazardous and should not be left to dangle. Medications and daily toiletries are definitely most convenient placed near the sink, as are soap and face cloths, toothbrushes and glasses.

Certainly, custom designed cupboards are the most efficient and harmonious storage. Beyond conventional bathroom cabinetry, improvised solutions can spark the bathroom. Rescued from other rooms, an antique mahogany buffet or small pine dresser will provide lots of attractive storage. An artist's taboret is ideal for cosmetics and hair pins, while handwoven baskets hold cakes of soap in reserve. And compared to the medicine-cabinet-with-fluorescent-light, a handsome wood cupboard or open shelving, beveled mirror, and adjustable lighting are truly more user-friendly.

A pine dry sink is used as a storage area in this English county bath. Almost dwarfing the piece is an immense ornamental framed mirror.

This magnificent, heavy leaded glass cupboard was salvaged from a large hall stand. In this bathroom it adds a practical and stylish touch.

Space in this long, narrow bathroom is utilized to the full with the slender enameled table and rows of glass shelving. In an area too limited to put in closed storage, an orderly, open arrangement falls short of seeming cluttered.

STORAGE

Architect Steven Holl's storage solution for this Manhattan apartment demonstrates the potential of custom cabinetry. Using only blue-gray and black, he created an abstract grid of functional units decorative enough to enhance any wall.

Towels are stored in open shelving between the bed and bath areas of Bromley-Jacobson's Manhattan loft. A glass wall separates the step-down shower with a recessed ceiling shower head. The storage shelf is placed so that it can be reached conveniently from both bed and bath areas.

*T*his 1930's bath in a Milanese flat, designed by Architect Rosanna Monzini employs new fixtures, original black marble surfaces, and a keenly rational use of storage. Large, framed mirrors double the space in the storage corridor outside.

*I*n keeping with the general simplicity of style, the storage area in the bath itself is limited to a single glass shelf above the sink. Everything else necessary is kept in the nearby spacious storage corridor/dressing area.

STORAGE

*T*owels are stored neatly under the
sink in this exposed unit that is covered
in ceramic tile. Towels and linens can
inject rotating color into a bathroom
when stored on open shelves.

*E*ven the drawer fronts are encased
in sumptuous onyx in this luxury bath,
where the sight of toiletries collecting
on surfaces would detract from the simplicity and extravagance of the onyx.

*A*rchitect Frank Gehry's witty storage solution is this recessed window
frame medicine chest. Deliberately
keeping an unfinished look to the wood
he replaced the sliding glass panes
with mirror.

*C*alifornia architects Morphosis used
custom wood and black laminate cabinetry throughout this long bathroom
connecting master bedroom and hallway. Only the sink breaks the lines
of the deep wooden drawers. The glass
block wall sheds diffuse light onto a
recessed shower area.

MIRRORS

It's a rare bathroom that has no mirror; even the most diffident person resorts to one for basic grooming. Invariably a small shaving mirror on an extendable arm or a more decorative three-sided frame mirror will be positioned over the sink. In this role, the selection should be made in conjunction with the lighting. For the best image, the mirror should be evenly lit from the sides. Light should be directed toward the face, not the mirror. Extendable magnifying mirrors combine simplicity and utilitarianism that can make them indispensible, but they function best as auxiliaries to a central mirror.

Beyond their purely functional role, mirrors add light, dimension, and a sense of spaciousness to a bathroom. The beauty of the medium is its versatility and effectiveness, whether used individually or as a floor-to-ceiling wallcovering.

A mirrored wall is dramatic and expansive, but it is relentlessly honest and not to everyone's taste. Smoked, tinted, or gold vein mirrors will subdue its frankness somewhat. Used architecturally, mirrors can serve equally to conceal unsightly areas or to multiply and underline interesting details as well as maximize light.

A hall of mirrors effect was created in a small bathroom in this San Francisco Arts and Crafts style house, by Osburn Design. Bird's-eye maple half-rounds define the arched mirror areas.

*M*irrors can be the most decorative bathroom essential. This Art Nouveau copper-framed mirror echoes the sober Edwardian elegance of a London bathroom.

A custom-made circular mirror floating above an angular freestanding sink
and cone-shaped floor light describe a
solid geometry in this California bed-
and-bath. The quarter moon fluorescent light casts an even glow over the
mirror.

A splendid Victorian hinged and mirrored vanity reflects the authentic details of this turn of the century West
Coast house. A pair of petal-shaded wall
lights flank the washing area.

MIRRORS

*Mirrors as form as well as function;
these three are a geometry lesson in this
cool Italian bath.*

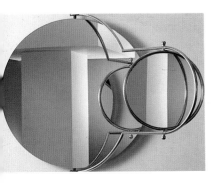

*I*rish designer Eileen Gray's satellite mirror, designed in 1926, has a supremely
practical swinging magnifying mirror.

*C*rooked shattered mirror, a glass whisk-
ered cat, and corrugated paper columns
make an unusually individualistic state-
ment in this London flat.

To any room, windows add a sense of space, blending the interior with the exterior world of shifting moods, seasons, and changing light. The Japanese, inspired perhaps by long soaks in their furos, often open the bathroom with expansive floor-to-ceiling windows that lead to secluded gardens. French windows and sliding glass doors invite the outdoors in, flooding the bathroom with sunlight and soft breezes.

Sadly, the bathroom window may seem almost an afterthought. Even when privacy is a prime factor, natural light should be extended as far as possible. Etched, frosted, stippled, and sand-blasted glass will be translucently private. Stained glass, whether saved from the wrecking ball or custom-designed, can create a beautiful feeling by adding light, colors, and camouflaging an imperfect world outdoors. Shoji screens, paper blinds, and gauze or lace will allow diffuse light, spreading it to corners. Mirror lining the frames of stingy windows will multiply light.

Glassblock, normally 6-inches square, can be used structurally to enlarge a window or replace clear glass panes for privacy. The blocks can be geometrically patterned, stippled, or translucent in varying degrees of opacity.

Skylights in the bathroom can need to be tempered. A roll-up shoji screen will shield intense sun when needed, while still flooding the room with diffused light.

The combination of sunlight and humidity is ideal for many kinds of plants. Settled into the window, geraniums, cacti, african violets, and many other houseplants will thrive in the bathroom.

Etched fish leap in swirls of foaming water in the rippled glass designed by William Morris. The message above the motif reflects the Victorian concept of the bath as a quasi-religious room for the purification of the body temple.

In this bath in a converted stone farm-house in France, only the glass in the arched windows delinates indoor from outdoor. The sunken tub is encased in the same rugged stone seen in the rock garden adjoining the bath. Plants fill the room, adding to the solarium effect created by the drama of the glass.

Stained glass offers privacy without diminishing the quality of light. The mosaic tiled surfaces of this Italian bath are washed in a pale colored light that penetrates the slender panels of floral patterned stained glass: even the ceiling catches the gleam.

*G*lass block makes an excellent bathroom window for the shimmering, watery light it throws upon a room, and of course, the privacy consideration. Here the glass becomes part of the tile pattern of the wall. The slant-back tub is also set in white tile, echoing the room's design scale.

*B*ars give a leaded glass effect to the open attic windows of this villa. The windows are high enough to ensure privacy and so are left uncovered. Below is a romantic sink treatment complete with candles, flowers, and bouquets stencilled onto the enameled walls.

*A*n ordinary window of pebbled glass becomes extraordinary through the ancient Japanese art of ikebana: *a celebration of the harmony of the natural line. Here twigs and lilies in an Art Deco vase fill the window sill, accompanied by two precisely placed shells, transforming the space into a meditation piece.*

DESIGN DIRECTORY

ASSOCIATIONS & FEDERATIONS

ACADEMIE D'ARCHITECTURE
HOTEL DES CHAULINES
9 Place des Vosges, 4E
75004 Paris
France

ACCENT ON INFORMATION
P.O. Box 700
Bloomington, IL 61701
*Information on products and special
devices that can make homes barrier free
for the disabled*

AMERICAN INSTITUTE OF
ARCHITECTS (AIA)
1735 New York Avenue NW
Washington, D.C. 20006

AMERICAN SOCIETY OF
INTERIOR DESIGNERS (ASID)
1430 Broadway
New York, NY 10018

ARCHITECTURAL ASSOCIATION
34-36 Bedford Square
London WC1
England

ASSOCIATION OF WOMEN IN
ARCHITECTURE
7440 University Drive
St. Louis, MO 63130

BUILDING CENTRE
26 Store Street
London WC1E 7BT
England

CONSIGLIO NAZIONALE
DEGLI ARCHITETTI
Corso Rinascimento 11
00186 Roma
Italy

DESIGN COUNCIL
THE DESIGN CENTRE
28 Haymarket Centre
London SW1Y 4FU
England

OFFICE OF ARCHAEOLOGY AND
HISTORICAL PRESERVATION
Dept. of the Interior
Washington, D.C. 20240

INTERNATIONAL COUNCIL
OF SOCIETIES OF INDUSTRIAL
DESIGN
45 Avenue Legrand
1050 Bruxelles
Belgium

INTERNATIONAL FEDERATION
OF INTERIOR DESIGNERS
Keizergracht 321
Amsterdam 1002
Netherlands

ISTITUTO NAZIONALE DI
ARCHITETTURA
Palazzo Taverna
Via Monte Giordano 36
00186 Roma
Italy

JAPAN INTERIOR DESIGN
ASSOCIATION
2-3-16 Gingumae
Shibuyaku, Tokyo
Japan

NATIONAL ASSOCIATION OF
HOME BUILDERS
15 M Street NW
Washington D.C. 20005

NATIONAL CENTER FOR A
BARRIER–FREE ENVIRONMENT
1140 Connecticut Avenue NW
Washington, D.C. 20036
Information resource for the disabled

NATIONAL KITCHEN & BATH
ASSOCIATION (NKBA)
124 Main Street
Hackettstown, NJ 07840

NATIONAL SAFETY CODES
425 N. Michigan Avenue
Chicago, IL 60611

ROYAL INSTITUTE OF BRITISH
ARCHITECTS (RIBA)
66 Portland Place
London W1N 4AD
England

STICHTING INDUSTRIELE
VORMGEVING
Beurs Damrak 62A
Amsterdam C
Netherlands

PUBLICATIONS & JOURNALS

ABITARE
EDITICE ABITARE SEGESTA s.p.a.
15 Corso Monforte, 20122
Milano
Italy

AIA JOURNAL
1735 New York Avenue, NW
Washington, D.C. 20006

ARCHITECTURAL DIGEST
4900 Wilshire Blvd.
Los Angeles, CA 90036

ARCHITECTURAL RECORD
1221 Avenue of the Americas
New York, NY 10020

ARCHITECTURAL REVIEW
9 Queen Ann's Gate
Westminster
England

ARCHITECTURE & URBANISM
30-8 Yushima 2 Chome
Buskyo-Ku, Tokyo 113
Japan

ARCHITECTURE D'AUJOURD'HUI
17 Rue D'Uzes
75002 Paris
France

ART AND ARCHITECTURE
1147 South Hope Street
Los Angeles, CA 90015

CASA VOGUE
Piazza Castello 27
20121 Milan
Italy

DESIGN & ENVIRONMENT
6400 Goldsboro Road
Washington, D.C. 20034

DESIGN INTERNATIONAL
Kaufering S7,
5330 Koeningswenker
West Germany

DESIGN MAGAZINE
28 Haymarket
London SW14 4SU
England

DESIGNERS WEST
8564 Melrose Avenue
Los Angeles, CA 90069

DOMUS
Viale de Chisallo 20
20151 Milan
Italy

GLOBAL ARCHITECTURE
3-12-14 Sendagaya, Shibuya-Ku
Tokyo
Japan

IDEA MAGAZINE
5 Nishikicho 1-Chrome
Kanda Chi Yodaku, Tokyo
Japan

IL BAGNO
PEG
Via Fratelli Bressan 2
20126 Milan
Italy

ID MAGAZINE OF INTERNATIONAL
DESIGN
330 W. 42nd Street
New York, NY 10036

INTERIOR DESIGN
850 Third Avenue
New York, NY 10022

INTERIORS: FOR THE CONTRACT
DESIGN PROFESSIONAL
BILLBOARD PUBLICATIONS, INC.
1515 Broadway
New York, NY 10036

INTERNI
Via Privata Goerlich 1
20037 Paderno Dugnano
Italy

JAPAN INTERIOR DESIGN INTERIA
1-22 Yotsuya
Shinjuku-ku Tokyo 760
Japan

MAISON ET JARDIN
4 Place du Palais Bourbon
75341 Paris
France

PROGRESSIVE ARCHITECTURE
Box 95759
Cleveland, OH 44101

THE WORLD OF INTERIORS
228-230 Fulham Road
London SW10 9NB
England

FIXTURES & FITTINGS

AMERICAN STANDARD
U.S. PLUMBING PRODUCTS
P.O. Box 2033
New Brunswick, N.Y. 08903
Manufacturer

AQUA-BATHS
351 West Broadway
New York, NY 10013
Retailer
Customized whirlpool tubs and spas
with fittings from international sources

AQUA GLASS
P.O. Box 412
Industrial Park
Adansville, TN 38310
Retailer, manufacturer

AQUARIUS INDUSTRIES, INC.
6401 Centennial Blvd.
Nashville, TN 37290
Manufacturer, retailer
Acrylic tubs, shower modules, whirlpools

ARTISTIC BRASS
N.I. INDUSTRIES, INC.
4100 Ardmore Avenue
South Gate, CA 90280
Manufacturer
Faucets and decorative accessories

ATHENIAN MARBLE
Box 488
Bethany, OK 73008
Manufacturer
Marble bathtubs and sinks

AUBURN BRASS DIVISION OF
AMEROCK CORPORATION
2501 West 5th Street
Santa Ana, CA 92703
Manufacturer
Decorative fittings, faucets, cabinet
hardware

A. BALL PLUMBING SUPPLY
1703 West Burnside Street
Portland, OR 97209
Manufacturer

BARCLAY PRODUCTS
P.O. Box 12257
Chicago, IL 60012
Mail-order
Reproductions of Victorian and turn of
century claw foot bathtubs, towel racks,
and various fittings

BATHS INTERNATIONAL, INC.
89 Fifth Avenue
New York, NY 10003
New York showroom for Kohler,
American Standard and other
manufacturers

BENJAMIN MANUFACTURING
CORPORATION
15 324 Illinois Avenue
Paramount, CA 90723
Manufacturer
Sinks and bathtubs designed to with-
stand hard treatment

CENTURION SENSATIONS
VERMAX CORPORATION
660 West 3560 South
Salt Lake City, UT 84119
Manufacturer

GUSTAVSBERG USA

CHICAGO FAUCET COMPANY
2100 South Nuclear Drive
Des Plaines, IL 60018
Manufacturer
Full line of fittings

COLTON WARTSILA, INC.
7120 Havenhurst Avenue, Suite 214
Van Nuys, CA 91406
Manufacturer
Scandia Water Closet, a water-saving toilet, plus a complete line of sinks, tubs, whirlpools, toilets, bidets

PATRICK CREEK CORPORATION
P.O. Box 135
Hindesburg, VT 05461
Retailer
Water-saving toilets and fittings

DOMESTIC ENVIRONMENTAL ALTERNATIVES
P.O. Box 1020
Murphy, CA 95247
Manufacturer
Antique fixtures, composting toilets

ELJER PLUMBINGWARE
Three Gateway Center
Pittsburgh, PA 15222
Manufacturer
Bathtubs, whirlpools, single and double toilets

ELKAY MANUFACTURING CORPORATION
2222 Camden Court
Oak Brook, IL 60521
Manufacturer
Stainless steel sinks, faucets

ENVIRONMENTAL RESTORATION & DESIGN (ERD)
2140 San Pablo Avenue
Berkeley, CA 94702
Manufacturer
Period porcelain fixtures, including reproduction pedestal sinks, pull-chain toilets, soap dishes

FIAT PRODUCTS
1 Michael Court
Plainview, NY 11803
Manufacturer
Acrylic bathing steamsuites, whirlpools, bathtubs, showers

AUBURN BRASS

FROGDESIGN
HARMUT ESSLINGER, INC.
34 South 2nd Street
Campbell, CA 95008
Importer
Designer, West German bath and shower fittings

GLASTEC DIVISION OFFICE
P.O. Box 28
Middlebury, IN 46540
Manufacturer
Acrylic/fiberglass tubs, whirlpools and spas

GROHE AMERICA
2677 Coyle Avenue
Elk Grove Village, IL 60007
Manufacturer
Sink and bathtub fittings, shower systems

GRUBER
25636 Avenue Stanford
Valencia, CA 91355
Manufacturer
Tubs for two, rectangular and oval tubs, whirlpools with back and head-rests, sinks

FIXTURES & FITTINGS

P.E. GUERIN, INC.
23 Jane Street
New York, NY 10014
Manufacturer
Louis XV, Empire, Louis XVI style hardware and fittings

GUSTAVSBERG, USA, INC.
3129 Pinewood Drive
Arlington, TX 76010
Retailer, manufacturer

HASTINGS TILE & IL BAGNO
COLLECTION
201 East 57th Street
New York, NY 10022
Manufacturer, importer
Large collection of tubs, showers, toilets, faucets, shower heads, cabinets, mirrors, accessories, as well as a full line of fittings

HEAD'S UP, INC.
14452 Franklin Avenue
Tustin, CA 92680
Manufacturer
Oak furnishings, including toilet seats, medicine cabinets, oak-framed mirrors

HYDRO-SPA
P.O. Box 429
Piru, CA 93040
Manufacturer
Hydro-spas and bathtubs

IRONMONGER MODERN
HARDWARE
1822 North Sheffield Avenue
Chicago, IL 60614
Importer
Representative for European wash basin consoles, and HEWI hardware, shower rails, grab rails

KALLISTA
DAVIS & WARSHOW, INC.
150 East 58th Street
New York, NY 10155
Importer
Imported fittings, especially shower, sink, bath faucets

KOHLER CO.
Kohler, WI 53044
Manufacturer

KROIN ARCHITECTURAL
COMPLEMENTS
14 Stony Street
Cambridge, MA 02138
Manufacturer
Fixtures and fittings

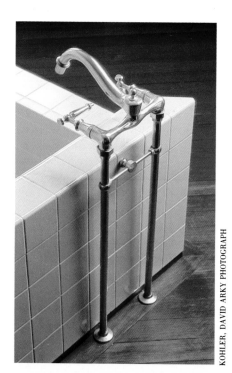

KOHLER, DAVID ARKY PHOTOGRAPH

LIPPERT CORPORATION
P.O. Box 219
Menomonee Falls, WI 53051
Manufacturer
Marble vanities, sinks, tubs, whirlpools

MOEN
STANADYNE
Elyria, OH 44036
Manufacturer
Sink, showers, tubs; new riser faucets
movable to different heights

NI INDUSTRIES
700 Fairway Drive
Walnut, CA 91789
Manufacturer

PAUL ASSOCIATES
42-05 10th Street
Long Island City, NY 11101
Manufacturer
Faucets of brass, chrome, acrylic, semi-
precious stone

PHILIPS INDUSTRIES, INC.
LASCO DIVISION
3261 East Miraloma Avenue
Anaheim, CA 92806
Manufacturer
Acrylic/fiberglass tub and shower units

PORCHER, INC.
507-2 North Wells Street
Chicago, IL 60610
Manufacturer
Sleek china baths, cast iron baths,
water-saving toilets

RESTORATION WORKS, INC.
P.O. Box 486
Buffalo, NY 14205
Manufacturer
Plumbing materials and fittings

SANYMETAL PRODUCTS
COMPANY, INC.
1705 Urbane Road
Cleveland, OH 44112
Manufacturer
Commercial hardware and fittings

SEPCO INDUSTRIES, INC.
491 Wortman Avenue
Brooklyn, NY 11208
Manufacturer
Brass, washerless, decorative faucets

YVONNE SHORT
5785 Arapahoe, F
Boulder, CO 80303
Designer
Custom porcelain sinks

SOFT BATHTUB COMPANY
P.O. Box 81125
Seattle, WA 98108
Manufacturer, distributor
Complete line of standard and oversized
bathtubs and institutional bathing
units

SPEAKMAN COMPANY
P.O. Box 191
Wilmington, DE 19899
Manufacturer
Polished brass and satin chrome fittings

SUNRISE SPECIALTY & SALVAGE
COMPANY
2210 San Pablo Avenue
Berkeley, CA 94702
Manufacturer, retailer
Elegant, historically accurate, Victorian-
style claw foot bathtubs, pull-chain
toilets with solid oak tanks, all brass
fittings

FIXTURES &
FITTINGS

U.S. TAP
P.O. Box 369
Frankfort, IN 46041
Manufacturer
Washerless faucets

TAYLOR INDUSTRIES
Anderson Road
Parkerford, PA 19457
Manufacturer
*Cultured marble in scalloped and oval
sinks, tubs, hydrotherapeutic whirlpool
massage systems*

THERMA SOL
Therma Sol Plaza
Leonia, NJ 07605
Manufacturer
*Whirlpool baths, steam showers,
portable spas*

USG CORPORATION
101 South Wacker Drive
Chicago, IL 60606-4385
Manufacturer
*Kinkead tub and shower doors; walls,
flooring, durock tile backer board
for walls in high moisture areas*

HASTINGS TILE, IL BAGNO COLLECTION

SHERLE WAGNER
INTERNATIONAL
60 East 54th Street
New York, NY 10022
Retailer, manufacturer

WATER CONSERVATION SYSTEMS
Damonmill Square Suite 41A
Concord, MA 01742
Importer
Water-saving and compost toilets

WATERCOLORS
Garrison-on-Hudson
New York, NY 10524
*Importer of Rubinetterie Zazzeri bath-
room fittings for wash basins, bathtubs,
bidets*

WESTERN BUILDERS CO-OP
ENVIRONMENTAL CONCERN
2150 Pine Drive
Prescott, AZ 86301
Importer
*Cascade plumbing fixtures from Sweden,
water closets, bidets, sinks*

HOT TUBS, SAUNAS, WHIRLPOOLS

JACUZZI WHIRLPOOL

AMEREC CORPORATION
P.O. Box 3825
Belleverne, WA 98009
Manufacturer
Steam bath generators and saunas

BAJA INDUSTRIES, INC.
4065 North Romero Road
Tucson, AZ 85705
Manufacturer
Indoor/outdoor spas

BLAZING SHOWERS
P.O. Box 327
Point Arena, CA 95468
Manufacturer
Alternate energy water heaters

CALIFORNIA COOPERAGE
P.O. Box E
San Luis Obispo, CA 93406
Manufacturer
Recreational tubs, spas, saunas

FORT WAYNE POOLS, INC.
510 Sumpter Drive
Fort Wayne, IN 46804
Manufacturer
Decorative spas

GORDON & GRANT
423 North Quarantina Street
Santa Barbara, CA 93103
Manufacturer
Redwood hot tubs

HYDRO-SPA
C/O HERR AND ASSOCIATES
4911 Warner Avenue Suite 208
Huntington Beach, CA 92649
Manufacturer
Whirlpools with command control

JACUZZI WHIRLPOOL BATH
298 North Wiget Lane
Walnut Creek, CA 94596
Manufacturer
Full line whirlpool supplier

JACUZZI WHIRLPOOL BATHS
THE PACIFIC GROUP
505 Sansome Street Suite 901
San Francisco, CA 94111
Manufacturer
Whirlpool baths, one person to multi-person whirlpool spas, completely portable whirlpools

WATERJET

KIMSTOCK, INC.
2200 South Yale Street
Santa Ana, CA 92704
Manufacturer
Whirlpool and shower bathing modules, portable spas

MACLEVY PRODUCTS CORPORATION
43-23 91st Place
Elmhurst, NY 11373
Manufacturer, importer
Full line of exercise equipment recreational tubs, saunas for professional and home use

HOT TUBS, SAUNAS, WHIRLPOOLS

McCOY, INC.
26630 Southfield Road
Southfield, MI 48076
Manufacturer
Kiln-dried western red cedar saunas,
steambaths, exercise equipment

MR. STEAM
AUTOMATIC STEAM PRODUCTS
CORPORATION
43-20 34th Street
Long Island City, NY 11101
Manufacturer
Steam bath generator systems for
residential and commercial use

STEAMIST COMPANY
1 Altman Drive
Rutherford, NJ 07070
Manufacturer
Steam baths, saunas, accessories

CALIFORNIA COOPERAGE

THERMA SOL
Therma Sol Plaza
Leonia, NJ 07605
Manufacturer
Whirlpool baths, steam showers,
portable spas

UNIVERSAL FITNESS PRODUCTS
(VIKING LEISURE PRODUCTS OF
NEW YORK)
20 Terminal Drive South
Plainview, NY 11803
Manufacturer
Whirlpools, saunas, steam baths

VIKING SAUNA COMPANY
HEALTH & LEISURE PRODUCTS
P.O. Box 76121
Atlanta, GA 30358
Manufacturer
Saunas, whirlpools, baths, spas

WATERJET
8431 Canoga Avenue
Canoga Park, CA 91304
Manufacturer
High tech whirlpools with computerized
comfort controls panel

WHIRL SPA, INC.
5320 NW 10th Terrace
Fort Lauderdale, FL 33309
Manufacturer
Hydrotherapy spas, bathtubs

DESIGNS FOR THE DISABLED

AMPCO PRODUCTS, INC.
7795 West 20th Avenue
Hialeah, FL 33014
Manufacturer
Cabinetry

ELJER PLUMBINGWARE
Three Gateway Center
Pittsburgh, PA 15222
Manufacturer
Bathtubs, whirlpools, single and
double toilets

**IRONMONGER MODERN
HARDWARE**
1822 North Sheffield Avenue
Chicago, IL 60614
Importer
Representative for European wash basin
consoles, and HEWI hardware, shower
rails, grab rails

**KROIN ARCHITECTURAL
COMPLEMENTS**
14 Stony Street
Cambridge, MA 02138
Manufacturer
Fixtures and fittings

**MASONITE CORPORATION
COMMERCIAL DIVISION**
Dover, OH 44622
Manufacturer
Full line of commercial bathroom
hardware

PRESSALIT, INC.
391 Main Street
Poughkeepsie, NY 12601
Importer
Well-designed sinks, toilets, and fittings

SOFT BATHTUB CO

HEWI/IRONMONGER

TUBULAR SPECIALTIES MFG., INC.
13011 South Spring Street
Los Angeles, CA 90961-1685
Manufacturer
Safety grab bars, shower and bath
seats, ramp safety railings, kick plates

UNIVERSAL RUNDLE
P.O. Box 29
New Castle, PA 16103
Manufacturer
Fixtures and fittings

ANTIQUES

STRUCTURAL ANTIQUES, INC.
1406 NW 30th Street
Oklahoma City, OK 73106
Architectural elements: doors, windows, columns, posts, lights

ARCHITECTURAL ANTIQUES
715 North Second Street
Philadelphia, PA 19123
Recovered bathroom fixtures

DEMOLITION AND SALVAGE
PELNIK WRECKING COMPANY, INC.
1749 Erie Blvd. East
Syracuse, NY 13210
Artifacts in stone, wood and cast iron, used bricks, fixtures, period radiators

SUNRISE SALVAGE

GARGOYLES, LTD.
512 South Third Street
Philadelphia, PA 19147

GREAT AMERICAN SALVAGE
3 Main Street
Montpelier, VT 05602
Wide-ranging, constant supply of recovered fixtures and fittings

IRREPLACEABLE ARTIFACTS
1046 Third Avenue
New York, NY 10021
International salvage from elegant residential and office buildings Victorian to 1950s

JOHN KREUSEL
R.R. 6
Rochester, MN 55901
Victorian through 1940s: truly vintage toilets, bathroom fixtures, accessories, lights

LOST CITY ARTS
257 West 10th Street
New York, NY 10014
Exceptional sinks, especially marble, and architectural elements

GREAT AMERICAN SALVAGE

SALVAGE ONE
1524 South Pedria Street
Chicago, IL 60608
Good selection of sinks, hardware, door knobs, windows

SUNRISE SPECIALTY & SALVAGE
COMPANY
2210 San Pablo Avenue
Berkeley, CA 94702
*Manufacturer and Retailer
Elegant, historically accurate, Victorian-style claw foot bathtubs, pull-chain toilets with solid oak tanks, all brass fittings*

TENNESSEE TUBS
905 Church Street
Nashville, TN 37203
Cast iron, roll rimmed, porcelain glazed tubs, pedestal lavatory sinks, pull-chain toilets

URBAN ARCHAELOGY LTD.
137 Spring Street
New York, NY 10012
Architectural fixtures from turn of century NYC bathrooms

EXERCISE EQUIPMENT

THE SHARPER IMAGE

MACLEVY PRODUCTS
CORPORATION
43-23 91st Place
Elmhurst, NY 11373
*Barbells, bicycle machines, boxing
equipment, treadmills, massage tables,
mats, rowing machines, saunas,
whirlpools*

NORDIC FITNESS PRODUCTS
89 Fifth Avenue
New York, NY 10003
Retailer
*Treadmills, massage benches, rowing
machines, exercise bicycles*

SHARPER IMAGE COMPANY
680 Davis Street
San Francisco, CA 94111
*Mail order catalog of extensive exercise
equipment and unusual accessories*

WORLD FAMOUS
4850-B Cass
San Diego, CA 92109
Manufacturer
Collapsible exercise equipment

BATH PRODUCT SUPPLIERS

THE SHARPER IMAGE

CAMBRIDGE CHEMISTS
702 Madison Avenue
New York, NY 10021
Mail order catalog
*Fine domestic and imported cosmetics,
beauty products, toiletries*

CRABTREE & EVELYN
30 East 67th Street
New York, NY 10021
Mail order catalog

DANS UN JARDIN
143 East 57th Street
New York, NY 10022
Retailer
Perfumes, soaps, eau de toilette

KIEHLE'S PHARMACY
109 Third Avenue
New York, NY 10003
Retailer
*Full line of homeopathic remedies,
herbal facials, botanical drugs, potions,
ointments, drugs—from natural products
exclusively*

FINISHING & SURFACING MATERIALS

A.C. MARBLE
P.O. Box 190
Ashland, KY 41105-4793
Manufacturer
Marble tubs, columns, showers

AMERICAN OLEAN TILE
Lansdale, PA 19446
Manufacturer
Ceramic tiles for countertops, walls, floors

ANDERSON CORPORATION
Bayport, MN 55003
Manufacturer
Windows and sliding doors

ARCHITECTURAL EMPHASIS, INC.
2743 9th Street
Berkeley, CA 94710
Manufacturer
Beveled glass panels

ARCHITECTURAL SCULPTURE
242 Lafayette Street
New York, NY 10012
Manufacturer
Plaster pieces, corbels, capitals

ARKANSAS WOOD DOORS, INC.
2404 Honeysuckle Lane
Russellville, AK 72801
Manufacturer
Custom doors from ash, oak, alder

ARM STAR
Department 201
P.O. Box 820, Industrial Blvd.
Lenon City, TN 37771
Manufacturer
Cast stone floor tiles and wall panels

ARMSTRONG WORLD INDUSTRIES
P.O. Box 3001
Lancaster, PA 17604
Manufacturer
Vinyl sheet floors, cast stone floor tiles, and wall panels

ART IN GLASS
779 Coney Island Avenue
Brooklyn, NY 11218
Manufacturer
Frosted, curved, beveled, sandblasted, etched glass

CASERTA CERAMICS
8106-8108 18th Avenue
Brooklyn, NY 11214
Importer
Cerdisc tile from Italy

CHERRY CREEK ENTERPRISES
937 Santa Fe Drive
Denver, CO 80204
Manufacturer
Beveled glass and stone wheel engravings

COUNTRY FLOORS
300 East 61st Street
New York, NY 10021
Importer
Hand-painted/hand-made ceramic tiles from Holland, Portugal, France, Spain, Italy, Mexico, Peru

DAVID AND DASH
2445 North Miami Avenue
Miami, FL 33137
Manufacturer
Fine fabrics, mass produced and custom-made

DIBIANCO IMPORTS
8018 Third Avenue
Brooklyn, NY 11209
Importer
Glass tiles, lamps, fixtures, fittings

DISH IS IT
2325 Third Street
Suite 410
San Francisco, CA 94107
Distributor
Hand-painted ceramic tile

E.I. DU PONT DE NEMOURS
Wilmington, DE 19898
Manufacturers
Corian

FABRICATIONS
145 East 56th Street
New York, NY 10022
Retailer
Imported cottons and other fabrics,
especially French prints

FOCAL POINT, INC.
2005 Marietta Road NW
Atlanta, GA 30318
Manufacturer
Mouldings, medallions, domes, rims,
cornices

FORMICA LAMINATES

FORMICA LAMINATE
10155 Reading
Cincinnati, OH 45241
Manufacturer
Colorcore surfacing materials

GABBIANELLI
201 East 57th Street
New York, NY 10155
Importer
Tiles from Italy

GALLERY OF APPLIED ARTS
24 West 57th Street
New York, NY 10019
Retailer
Artists' textiles, tiles, furniture

HAMILTON ADAMS IMPORTS, LTD.
P.O. Box 2489
Secaucus, NJ 07094
Manufacturer
Natural fiber wallcoverings

INSUL SHUTTER/FIRST LAW
PRODUCTS, INC.
P.O. Box 888
Keene, NH 03431
Manufacturer
Insulated shutters

INTEGRITY TILE COMPANY
The Marketplace
2400 Market Street
Philadelphia, PA 19103
Importer
Ceramic tiles and marble stone

DISH IS IT

ITALIAN TILE CENTER
499 Park Avenue
New York, NY 10022
Importer
Wide selection of ceramic tile

J & R LAMB STUDIOS
30 Joyce Drive
Spring Valley, NY 10977
Manufacturer
Custom-designed, leaded, stained-glass
windows

JASON/PIRELLI
340 Kaplan Drive
Fairfield, NJ 07006
Manufacturer
Rubber flooring

FINISHING & SURFACING MATERIALS

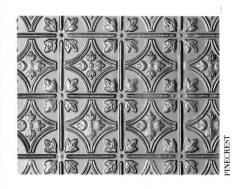

PINECREST

MARBLE TECHNICS, LTD.
150 East 58th Street
New York, NY 10155
Manufacturer
Tiles of marble, granite, stone

MID-STATE TILE
P.O. Box 1777
Lexington, NC 27292
Manufacturer
*Quarry and terra cotta tiles, glazed
and unglazed*

**MONARCH
MIRROR DOOR COMPANY, INC.**
21325 Superior Street
Chatsworth, CA 91311
Manufacturer
Mirrors and mirrored doors

MONARCH TILE MANUFACTURING
P.O. Box 2041
San Angelo, TX 76902
Manufacturer, importer
Ceramic wall and floor tiles

**MOULTRIE MANUFACTURING
COMPANY**
P.O. Drawer 1179
Moultrie, GA 31768
Manufacturer
*Decorative aluminum columns, lamps,
furniture in cast iron*

NEVAMAR CORPORATION
8339 Telegraph Road
Odenton, MD 21113
Manufacturer
Floor coverings and decorative laminates

NORA FLOORING
4201 Wilson Avenue
Madison, IN 47250
Manufacturer
Synthetic rubber flooring

**OLD WORLD
MOULDING AND FINISHING, INC.**
115 Allen Blvd.
Farmingdale, NY 11735
Manufacturer
Wood mouldings and finishings

PINECREST, INC.
2118 Blaisdell Avenue
Minneapolis, MN 55404
*Full line of shutters, shoji screens, and
tin ceilings*

MOULTRIE MANUFACTURING COMPANY

PIONEER PLASTICS
Box 1014, Pionite Road
Auburn, ME 04210-1014
Manufacturer

RAMBUSCH
40 West 13th Street
New York, NY 10011
Manufacturer
*Architectural glass and original stained-
glass designs*

ROMARCO
P.O. Box 2218
Morganton, NC 28655
Manufacturer
Cultured marble

SIMPLEX CEILING CORPORATION
50 Harrison Street
Hoboken, NJ 07030
Manufacturer
*Acoustical and non-acoustical aluminum
ceilings and wall coverings*

TARKETT, INC.
P.O. Box 128
Vails Gate, NY 12584
Manufacturer
Asbestos-free sheet vinyl and floor tiles

LIGHTING

DAVID AND DASH

VILLEROY AND BOCH
Interstate 80 at New Maple Avenue
Pine Brook, NJ 07058
Manufacturer
Glazed, unglazed, extruded tiles

VINTAGE LUMBER AND
CONSTRUCTION COMPANY
Route 1
Box 194
Frederick, MD 21701
Manufacturer
*Post and beam structures, hardwood
flooring*

WILSON ART
1 Brenner Drive
Congers, NY 10920
Manufacturer
Chemical-resistant laminates

TILE SHOP
1005 Harrison Street
Berkeley, CA 94710
Manufacturer, importer
Porcelain, German granite tiles

VERMONT MARBLE COMPANY
61 Main Street
Proctor, VT 05765
Manufacturer

VERMONT STRUCTURAL SLATE
COMPANY, INC.
Box 98
Fair Haven, VT 05743
Manufacturer
Interior slate flooring, vanity tops

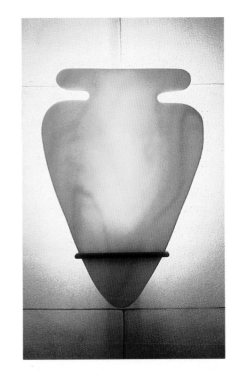

AAMSCO MANUFACTURING, INC.
P.O. Box 15119
Jersey City, NJ 07305
Manufacturer
Incandescent lighting

AMERICAN GLASS LIGHT
COMPANY
37 West 72nd Street
New York, NY 10023
Manufacturer
Deco style lighting

ARTEMIDE
150 East 58th Street
New York, NY 10155
Trade showroom
Italian lighting and furnishings
Access only via architect or designer

ATELIER INTERNATIONAL, LTD.
595 Madison Avenue
New York, NY 10022
Trade showroom
European lighting and other furnishings
Access only via architect or designer

BIEFFEPLAST
227 West 17th Street
New York, NY 10011
Importer
Italian mirrors, lighting, furniture

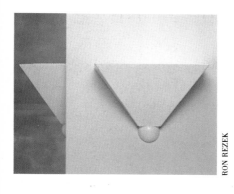

RON REZEK

BOYD LIGHTING COMPANY
56 12th Street
San Francisco, CA 94103-1293
Distributor
Modern lighting

THE FURNITURE CLUB
257 West 19th Street
New York, NY 10011
Designers
Lighting and other accessories

IPI
INNOVATIVE PRODUCTS FOR
INTERIORS
315 East 62nd Street
New York, NY 10021
Importer
Lighting and modern furniture

JUST BULBS
938 Broadway
New York, NY 10010
Retailer
Mail order catalog
Large selection of light bulbs:
nationwide

LES PRISMATIQUES, INC.
232 East 59th Street
New York, NY 10022
Retailer
One-of-a-kind and limited edition
lighting, other furnishings

LIGHTING SERVICES, INC.
150 East 58th Street
New York, NY 10155
Manufacturer
Track lighting

FURNITURE CLUB

METROPOLITAN LIGHTING
FIXTURE COMPANY, INC.
1010 Third Avenue
New York, NY 10021
Manufacturer

NOWELLS, INC.
490 Gate 5 Road
Sausalito, CA 94965
Retailer
Lighting, fixtures, antiques

RAMBUSCH LIGHTING
40 West 13th Street
New York, NY 10011
Manufacturer, Retailer
Deco style lighting, sconces

RON REZEK LIGHTING AND
FURNITURE
5522 Venice Blvd.
Los Angeles, CA 90019
Retailer
Halogen lighting

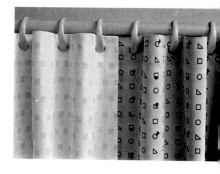

AD HOC SOFTWARES
410 West Broadway
New York, NY 10014
Retailer
Towels to shower curtains

ALLIBERT, INC.
Raritan Center, Building 423
100 Northfield Avenue
Edison, NJ 08837
Manufacturer
Polystyrene cabinets, mirrors, accessories

BALDWIN BRASS CENTER
210 East 60th Street
New York, NY 10022
Manufacturer
Architectural period styling in brass with
clear, baked enamel finish

BATHTIQUE INTERNATIONAL
247 North Goodman
Rochester, NY 14607
Retailer
Shower curtains, linens, and accessories

CANNON MILLS
1271 Sixth Avenue
New York, NY 10020
Manufacturer
Bath Linens

CUMBERLAND GENERAL STORE
Route 3
Crossville, TN 38555
Mail order catalog
Large selection of unusual turn of century bath fixtures, fittings, accessories, cabinet hardware

D.F. SANDERS & COMPANY
386 West Broadway
New York, NY 10012
Retailer
Streamlined accessories

FIELDCREST MILLS, INC.
60 West 40th Street
New York, NY 10018
Manufacturer
Bath Linens

HAMMACHER SCHLEMMER
147 East 57th Street
New York, NY 10022
Retailer
Mail order catalog
Extraordinary gadgets

HOFFRITZ INTERNATIONAL
515 West 24th Street
New York, NY 10011
Mail order catalog, retailer
Precision beauty and grooming accessories

JAMES HONG
146 West 29th Street
New York, NY 10001
Furniture designer

HORCHOW COLLECTION
P.O. Box 819066
Dallas, TX 75381-9066
Mail order catalog
Accessories for bathing and grooming

HYDRO-VALVE COMPANY
1310 Rockaway Parkway
Brooklyn, NY 11212
Manufacturer
Towel warmers

INTERNA DESIGNS LTD
The Merchandise Mart
Space 6-168
Chicago, IL 60654
Trade Showroom
Collection of imported furniture
Access only via an architect or designer

KROIN INCORPORATED
Charles Square, Suite 300
Cambridge, MA 02138
Importers
Fittings, lavatory faucets,
bath, shower fittings, accessories

JAMES HONG

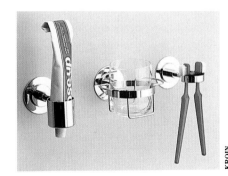

KROIN

THE HORCHOW COLLECTION

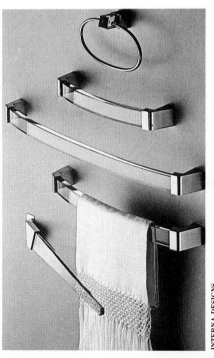

INTERNA DESIGNS

ACCESSORIES

**RALPH LAUREN HOME
FURNISHINGS, INC.**
1185 Avenue of the Americas
New York, NY 10036
Manufacturer
Bath Linens

LIMN
457 Pacific Avenue
San Francisco, CA 94133
Retailer
*Collection of international accessories
and furnishings*

MARTEX
1221 Avenue of the Americas
New York, NY 10020
Manufacturer
Bath Linens

**MIROIR BROT USA, INC.
THE FRENCH REFLECTION**
5555 South Sepulveda Blvd.
Culver City, CA 90230
Distributor
Mirrors

MIROIR BROT U.S.A.

MUSEUM SHOP
11 West 53rd Street
New York, NY 10019
Mail order catalog, retailer
*Houseware, hardware, reproductions
from the design collection of the Museum
of Modern Art*

MYSON, INC.
P.O. Box 5025 Falmouth
Fredricksburg, VA 22403
Manufacturer
*Towel warmers in floor-fixed and
wall-mounted units*

**NUTONE HOUSING
GROUP-SCOVILL**
Madison and Red Bank Roads
Cincinnati, OH 45227
Manufacturer
*Safety grab bars, towel racks, soap
holders, toothbrush holders, shelves,
paperholders*

PAUL ASSOCIATES
42-05 10th Street
Long Island City, NY 11101
Manufacturer
*Coordinated accessories: towel racks,
soap holders, toothbrush holders,
shelves, paperholders*

PEARL TEXTILE CO., INC.
1013 Grand Street
Brooklyn, NY 11211
Manufacturer
*Institutional and made-to-order woven
towels*

PORTHAULT, INC.
57 East 57th Street
New York, NY 10022
Distributor
Fine bath linens of natural fiber

PRATESI
829 Madison Avenue
New York, NY 10021
Distributor
Italian bath and table linens

GILLION SKELLENGER
715 West Briar Place
Chicago, IL 60657
Designer
Tiles and shower curtains

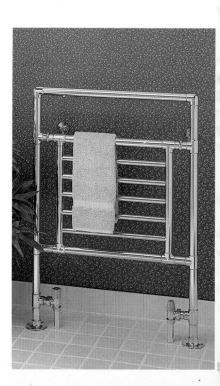

STORAGE

OINTU
0 East 69th Street
New York, NY 10021
Mail order catalog, retailer
International modern design, from
mass-produced to limited-edition pieces

ERRAILLON CORPORATION
5/Q South Hoffman Lane
Central Islip, NY 11722
Manufacturer
Rust-resistant scales in a variety
of finishes

THE ELEGANT JOHN
312 Lexington Avenue
New York, NY 10021
Retailer
Decorative accessories

VALLI & COLOMBO
P.O. Box 245
Duarte, CA 91010
Manufacturer
Door handles, latches, knobs, hooks in
brass and wood

WIFE OF BATH SHOPPE
45 Christopher Street
New York, NY 10014
Retailer
Bath accessories, linens, personalized
shower curtains

ART ET INDUSTRIE
594 Broadway
New York, NY 10013
Retailer
One-of-a-kind, limited edition pieces
from artists and designers

DIBARTOLOMEO WOODWORKING
986 Pratt Street
Philadelphia, PA 19124
Restoration and custom cabinetry

FURNITURE OF THE
TWENTIETH CENTURY
227 West 17th Street
New York, NY 10011
Retailer
Imports including Bieffeplast USA, the
Memphis collection and Andrée Putman's
Ecart line of reproduction classics

HANCOCK SHAKER VILLAGE
P.O. Box 898
Pittsfield, MA 01202
Manufacturer
Hand-made Shaker furniture and
accessories—mirrors, towel racks

ICF
INTERNATIONAL CONTRACT
FURNISHINGS
305 East 63rd Street
New York, NY 10021
Trade showroom with extensive collec-
tion of imported furniture, including
lacquered cabinetry
Access only via an architect or designer

HEWI/IRONMONGER

QUAKER MAID
A TAPPAN DIVISION
Route 61
Leesport, PA 19533
Manufacturer
Wall mounted cabinets in pine, oak,
cherry, pecan

RICHWOOD
A TAPPAN DIVISION
200 West Ottawa Street
Richwood, OH 43344
Manufacturer
Vanity door bases, linen cabinets,
hamper units, medicine cabinets

EUROPEAN
SOURCES

C.P. HART & SONS

A BIGGER SPLASH
119 Fulham Road
London SW3
England
Modern fixtures and fittings

AGAPE
46038 Frassino Mantovano/
Mantova/Italia
Zona Industriale
Via Pioner 2
Italy
Colorful bathroom cabinets

ALAPE
Adolf Lamprecht Betriebs-GmbH
D-3380 Goslar 1
West Germany
Bathroom accessories

ARCHITECTURAL HERITAGE
Boddington Manor
Boddington
Nr Cheltenham, Gloucestershire
England
*Victorian-style, floral decorated toilets
and sinks*

ARCOS
UFFICI E AMMINISTRAZIONE
95127 Catania-Via Teramo, 13
Italy
*Manufacturer
Elegant bathtubs*

ARMITAGE SHANKS SALES LTD
Armitage
Rugeley
Staffordshire WS15 4BT
England
*Leading manufacturer of bathroom
fixtures*

BATHROOM & SHOWER CENTRE
204 Great Portland Street
London W1N 6AT
England
*Showroom for Twyfords baths, sinks,
toilets*

**BEACON ARCHITECTURAL
SALVAGE AND THE DECO
BATHROOM**
Nr. Stratford-upon-Avon
England
*Edwardian 1920s and 1930s roll-top
baths, sinks, toilets, brass-nickel fittings*

BOFFI/PUNTO BAGNO
20030 Lentate Sul Seveso/Milano
Via Oberdan 70
Italy
*Sink units fitted into cone-shaped and
square vanities*

BONSACK BATHS LTD
14 Mount Street
London WI 5RA
England
*2000 colors, taps, accessories, mirrors,
lights; bathroom design and installation
worldwide*

BYGONE BATHROOM FITTINGS
No. 2 Outside Georgian Village
Camden Passage
London N1
England
*Antique and reproduction fittings and
fixtures*

CP HART & SONS LTD
Newnham Terrace, Hercules Road
London SE1 7DR
England
Reproduction tubs and accessories

AGAPE

CARRARA & MATTA
Sede: 10135 Torino
Via Onorato Vigliani, 24
Italy
Cabinets and accessories

CAZEAUX
15, Rue de Larreguy
64200 Biarritz-la Negresse
Pyrénées-Atlantique
France
Traditional tiles

CZECH & SPEAKE LTD.
39c Jermyn Street
London SW1
England
Traditional bathroom fixtures and fittings

DOMA LTD.
KITCHEN BATHROOM INTERIORS
110 Brompton Road
Knightsbridge, London SW3 1JJ
England

FRANÇOIS VERNIN
CARREAUX D'APT
Le Pont Julien
84400 Bonnieux, Vauchise
France
Country-style tiles

GIORGIO S.V.I.
Via Leonardo da Vinci, 43
20090 Trezzano S/N Italy
"Old American" porcelain sinks: decorative and ornate pedestals

GNUTTI SEBASTIANO &
FIGLI SPA
25065 Lumezzand S.S. (Brescia)
Via Montesnello 47
Italy
Chrome, brass, colored shower, sink, and tub fittings

HANSGROHE
Postfach
7622 Schiltach
West Germany
Modern showers and taps

HAVENPLAN'S ARCHITECTURAL
EMPORIUM
The Old Station, Station Road
Killamarsh Nr. Sheffield
England
Architectural antiques

HILL HOUSE INTERIORS
Rotunda Buildings
Montpellier Circus
Cheltenham, Gloucestershire
England
Victorian and Edwardian bathrooms and kitchens

IDEAL STANDARD LTD
P.O. Box 60
National Avenue
Hull HU5 4JE
England
Major manufacturer of bathroom fixtures

IOTTI S.P.A.
INDUSTRIA ARREDAMENTI PER
BAGNO
Via Carboni, 50
42010 Villaratti (Reggio Emilia)
Italy
Bathroom cabinets and accessories

LONDON ARCHITECTURAL
SALVAGE COMPANY
Mark Street
London EC2A 4ER
England

MAX PIKE'S BATHROOM SHOP
Unit 5/4 Eccleston Street
London SW1
England
Baths, sinks, toilets: faucets, showers, steambaths, jacuzzis: tiles, toilet seats

EUROPEAN SOURCES

METALPLASTICA LUCCHESE
55060 Nomsagrati (Lucca)
Italy
Modern, primary colored bathroom accessories: mirrors, towel rails, vanities

MOBELHAUS S.P.A.
Via Roma
20-42022 Broeho (Reggio Emilia)
Italy

ORAS OY
Box 40
SF-26101 Rauma
Finland
Shower, sink, bathtub fittings

ORIGINAL BATHROOMS
143-145 Kew Road
Richmond-upon-Thames
Surrey TW9 2PN
England
Large bathroom showroom, knowledgeably run by descendants of Humpherson, inventor of the wash-down toilet

PARIS CERAMICS
543 Battersea Park Road
London SW11
England
Antique, modern French, Spanish floor and wall tiles

PENHALIGON'S
41 Wellington Street
Covent Garden, London WC2
England
Elegant, traditional perfumery

POGGENPOHL U.K., LTD
Thames House
63 Kingston Road
New Malden
Surrey KT3 3PB England
Sleek, modern accessories and sinks

PRESSALIT
Dansk Pressalit A/S
Dungsten Borggade 11013
DK-8000 Aarhus C
Denmark
Well-designed sinks, toilets, and fittings

CZECH & SPEAKE

PROPERTYPLAN & PALACE BATHROOMS
33-35 Elystan Street
London SW3
England

ROYAL DOULTON
Whieldon Road
Stoke-on-Trent ST4 4 HN
England
Major manufacturer of bathroom fixtures

RUBINETTERIE STELLA S.P.A.
Via Unita D'Italia 1
28100 Novara
Italy
Taps for shower, bath, bidet

RUBINETTERIE TOSCANE PONSI S.P.A.
55049 Viareggio
Via Volta, 2
Italy
Shower, sink, bathtub fittings

RUSTIC 1
Via Per Sinalunga
52045 Foiano Della/Chiana
Italy
Wide variety of mirrors, soap dishes, waste baskets

S. POLLIACK, LTD
Norton Industrial Estate, Norton,
Malton
North Yorkshire YO17 9HQ
England
Decorative fittings and accessories

B.C. SANITAN
30-31 Lyme Street
London NW1
England
Antique design bathtubs and toilets

SITTING PRETTY
131 Dawes Road
London SW6
England
Traditional fittings, authentic and
reproduction; Victorian a specialty

TENAX
CERAMICA TENAX, S.P.A.
Via Cernobbio 5
20158 Milano
Italy
Streamlined and neoclassical bidets,
toilets

TEUCO
TEUCO GUZZINI SRL
Via Passionisti
62019 Recanti
Macerata
Italy
Leading manufacturer of modern tubs,
showers, sauna-showers, toilets, sinks
in almost every shape and size

TSE - TECHNIQUES AND
SYSTEMES ELABORES
77 Bis, Rue Michel-Ange
75016 Paris
France
Acrylic, enameled cast iron, enameled
steel whirlpool tubs; many shapes and
sizes

TUILLERIE FORGE
MAYLE-DAVID
Morizes
33190 La Reole, Gironde
France
Rustic French tiles

WATERFRONT LIMITED
3 Brookmead Industrial Estate
Jessops Way
Beddington Lane
Croydon, Surrey CRO 4TS
England
Exclusive Italian bathrooms

ORAS OY

WORKING WITH A PROFESSIONAL

WORKING WITH
A PROFESSIONAL

All new bathrooms and most re-modelled or renovated bathrooms are completed with some kind of professional assistance—from an architect, designer, contractor, and sometimes all three. Coordinating bathroom fixtures and fittings while concealing the mechanics of plumbing, electricity, ventilation, temperature and humidity control to achieve a comfortable, pleasant room makes the bathroom the greatest residential design challenge.

In many communities building codes stipulate professionally drawn plans or the involvement of licensed electricians, plumbers, and carpenters. But often people do feel concerned that an architect or designer will mean unnecessary expense or a loss of control. These premonitions are entirely understandable, but with consideration and planning, they will be unfounded. Instead, the professional's familiarity with fixtures and fittings, architectural elements and finishes, and the construction industry in general may actually mean a savings greater than his or her fee. Floor plans, construction drawings, specifications for materials, furnishings,

equipment, and methods of construction, will provide a uniform and economical basis for contract bids and the performance of the job.

To ensure this satisfactory result then, the architect or designer must clearly understand the project's functional and aesthetic requirements, even down to the position of the soap dish or the height of the mirror light. Designing or renovating a bathroom is complicated and the results will have to be lived with for sometime, so it is important to get the job right. For their years of training and experience, the architect and designer are prepared to ensure that this happens.

DESIGN FEES

Design professionals offer a variety of services for which they charge accordingly. It is possible to commission a brief consultation on a single aspect of the job to a total design, from the development of basic floor plans to overseeing the entire construction and decoration. Some architects and designers will request a fee for any consultation or initial interview, others only if they receive the commission. Fees can be an agreed-to sum or a percentage of the costs of the construction. Often designers will work on a sliding scale; that is, their commission percentage will decrease as the costs of the project rise. In any case, payments are usually scheduled at completion of specific phases of the work.

CHOOSING AN ARCHITECT OR DESIGNER

Many (but certainly not all) architects and designers belong to their respective national organizations, the American Institute of Architects (AIA) and the American Society of Interior Designers (ASID). Both AIA and ASID have local chapters across the country which also act as liaison with the public, recommending local professionals suited to a given project. AIA and ASID will supply without charge information about the commonly accepted tenets of the designer/client relationship, along with sample contracts and letters of agreement, price lists, and design synopses.

Personal recommendation is of course a time-honored means of selection. With the benefit of someone else's experiences and firsthand impressions of the results of that work, it is far easier to assess suitability for a project. Naturally this evidence has to be weighed carefully: friends' bathrooms or homes will reflect their own taste more than their architect's or designer's.

But it is the quality of the finishing and detailing—an imaginative use of a window area, an interesting approach to lighting, or a harmonious pairing of faucets with towel rail or both with the door handle, for example—that will often reveal more about a professional's work than the color of the walls or the shape of the bathtub.

Photographs of a particular architect's work can also help to find the right person. Pictures of bathrooms (or any other room) that includes specific fixtures or fittings or design, or that simply capture the right mood, will help to focus ideas and later to communicate with the architect or designer.

For major work it is quite normal and advisable to interview at least three architects or designers, sometimes more. In introductory interviews, the client should be prepared to explain something of the nature and extent of the job, so that the architect or designer can determine if it is appropriate. Initial interviews are traditionally tentative, so the client may feel difficulty conversing intelligently about the project. Several interviews on, a more firmly developed feeling for the various facets of the job will mean an enhanced sense of confidence, and it will be possible to be more explicit with designers.

These screening interviews with architects or designers serve several purposes. They give the client an opportunity to see portfolios and get to know each firm's work better. At this point general questions about experience, work procedures, and fees can be asked. But most important the client should look for an understanding or empathy concerning the job, without which a sense of trust in subsequent design decisions will become increasingly difficult.

The architect or designer/client relationship is an intimate one in nature. The design and decoration of our homes probably say more about our personalities and how we view ourselves than any other single thing. For any design to be successful, therefore, it must accurately capture aspects of our personality and interpret them into a tangible, functional form.

All the renderings, scale models, and philosophical statements by architects or designers cannot substitute for firsthand knowledge. Visiting completed jobs and talking with previous clients can provide valuable insights into both the type of work and the kind of working relationship a client should expect.

THE DESIGN PROCESS

The first step in developing a design is the written schematic or programming phase, during which the architect or designer gathers as much information about the client as possible: how he or she lives, what are the design expectations, and most importantly, the budgetary requirements. At this point the client should be as candid and straightforward as possible, and express likes and dislikes of the present (or other) bathroom even down to the smallest details. Specific comments about the existing design are most helpful. Is the bathroom too small or too dark? Is it 'unfriendly' or uncomfortable? Is there enough storage, or enough room to wash? The architect or designer will want to know how many peole will be using the bathroom, how often, and at what times; what activities should be incorporated into the layout; the particular grooming needs or privacy requirements; if the family will increase or diminish; how closely the bathroom should relate to its neighboring rooms; and so on.

The client should try to convey the mood and style for the room: should it be formal and spacious, eccentric and eclectic, or intimate and unimposing? Architectural styles are just as important in the bathroom as in any other room, and a preference for Art Nouveau or Art Deco, French Provincial or Biedermeier, should be voiced. Swatches of fabric, color samples, even an individual object such as a vase or piece of pottery can guide the designer.

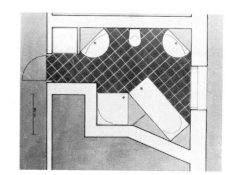

SCHEMATIC DRAWINGS

Once the requirements have been firmly established, the architect or designer can begin to translate these requirements into preliminary drawings that satisfy as many objectives as possible within the constraints of space and budget. These first sketches provide the basis for additional consultations with the client, when early solutions are accepted or rejected or modified, and as priorities and limitations in the design become apparent.

With the client's approval, the drawings are taken a stage further to more detailed plans that show the exact placement of fixtures and ideas for the colors, materials, and finishes in the room. Now the designer can begin to estimate the cost of the project. This figure is normally based on prevailing local construction costs as well as the cost of fixtures and materials. Permit fees, any special testing of materials or consultations, and inspections or reports required by law are likely to be extra. It is quite possible that this preliminary costing is

25 or even 50 percent above the original budget. But this plan should incorporate the ideal fulfillment of the client's original requirements. The kinds of design solutions and compromises that match this with the budget are frequently the most inventive and constructive. Ultimately, it may be that the building has to occur in phased stages, as finances permit, over several years.

At this point, however, nothing has been finalized and there is still room for consultation, criticism, and modification of the plans. Whenever an element in the design is unclear or seems inadequate, the client should ask about it. Perhaps the shower should be made larger and the storage area reduced, or a partition put in between the toilet and bathing areas. Changes in this early planning stage are far more easily accomplished than when construction has begun.

DESIGN DEVELOPMENT

Based on the client's approval of schematic drawings, design development drawings will be prepared. Documents at this point fix and describe the size and character of the interior construction for the project, including special features to be built into walls, floors, partitions, or ceilings. They also include data and illustrations for all fixtures and furnishings, including any specially designed items, to indicate the finished appearance of the bathroom. The designer will include recommendations for any colors, materials, and finishes not previously specified. A revised estimate of probable cost will be given, and at this point the design is set.

CONTRACT DOCUMENTS

Once the design development is approved, the designer or architect will begin to fine tune the project through the contract documents phase. The designer will prepare construction documents that consist of drawings, schedules, specifications, and any other documents necessary to set forth in detail the requirements of the construction. Thus the details of fabrication, procurement, shipment, delivery, and installation are established. The documents are submitted and approved by the proper government agency. (While the designer acts as the client's professional representative, the performance of the work commissioned through the design documents is the legal responsibility of the client.)

At this point the client will approach contractors and suppliers, or consider hiring a general contractor. The general contractor should obtain all necessary permits, hire and supervise subcontractors, schedule all phases of the work, coordinate bank and building inspections, and deal with the problems which invariably arise. (The homeowner who plans to act as general contractor should be knowledgeable about construction and have the time, patience, and detachment to supervise the work.) Clients interviewing prospective general contractors can ask to talk with their previous employers. Such points as satisfaction with the finished job, scheduling, problem solving, and budgeting are fair barometers of a contractor's sense of responsibility. Perhaps the most frequently heard advice will be: assume nothing, and get everything in writing.

The assistance of the architect or designer at this stage can be invaluable. The coordination of bidding and negotiating is complex and rattling. The selection of the contractor may be based on competitive bidding or by a process of recommendation, interview, and a negotiation for the contract. In competitive bidding, the designer provides drawings, specifications, and bidding forms to contractors so that they can submit their sealed bids within a given time. The low bid is usually awarded the contract. A negotiated contract may be based on a previous good working rapport or other recommendation. The contractor may be compensated with a fixed fee or a percentage of the construction costs. Guaranteed cost limits can be set and savings of cost or time encouraged by bonuses.

As with the selection of an architect or designer, at least three contractors should be interviewed; references should be checked, if not with previous clients, then certainly with the local consumer affairs department.

Negotiation without an architect or designer should proceed with care. Professional construction drawings and a materials list provide a sound economical basis for competitive bidding, insuring that all contractors are basing their bids on uniform information. Floorplans and sketches, together with a materials list that specifies particular types of products by brand name and construction methods will make comparison of bids easier.

Because of the complex nature of bathroom construction, the various elements of even a minor redecoration can combine to potentially awesome proportions. Painstaking planning will ease some of the inconvenience to the family. Realistic consideration is necessary if one is to do without the bathroom, and perhaps even to the water supply to the house; the number of workers who will have to be accommodated; the amount of storage space needed for construction materials and new fixtures; the effect of the construction on other rooms, are all important points to be settled before a schedule is drawn.

CONTRACTS ADMINISTRATION

The awarding of one or more contracts commences the contract administration phase for the designer. Throughout this period the designer acts as a representative of the client, visiting the site to ensure that work is on schedule and of proper quality. The designer will also act as a mediator between client and contractor in the event of minor conflicts. As the interpreter of the requirements of the approved contract documents, the designer is in charge of approving materials, fixtures, and equipment, and authorizes previously agreed on payments to the contractor.

Clients should be thoroughly aware of their legal responsibilities as set in the contract documents. Alterations in the design during construction should never be instrumented without first conferring with the designer. This would not only breach the contract, but could also result in changes for seemingly unaffected elements in the design or construction. A change in the specified size of a window, for instance,

could impinge on the installation of the surrounding storage cabinets already on order, as well as the granting of approval from local authorities over requisite ventilation of the room.

At the finish of the project, the client will conduct a walk-through inspection of the entire room with both the contractor and the designer. This inspection results in a 'punch list' of non-functioning items and corrections to be made in the workmanship. Final payments should be made after these corrections are completed.

A

Adam, Robert 101
Allen, Janet 98
Ambient Lighting 126
American Standard 102
Aqua Sulis 12
Artemide 124

B

The Bathroom Book 78
Bathtubs 110
Bed and Bath 66
Bernstein, Mel 36, 92
Biagiotti, Laura 31
Bidets 102
Bromley Jacobson 44, 104, 142
Brown, Ted 118
Burges, William 18, 19
Bute, Lord and Lady 15, 65

C

California Cooperage 116
Castle Coch 15
Catroux, Francois 38
Chapple, John 15

Children's Bathrooms 76
Colefax and Fowler 69
Corner Fixtures 70
Couples Bathrooms 58
Crane 26
Crapper, Thomas 100

D

Dansk Pressalit 80
D'Aquino, Carl 46
Dawson, Chris 114, 137
Del Rio, Delores 50
Disabled, Bathrooms For 78

E

Eltham Palace 26

F

Falconetto 34
Family Bathrooms 54
Faucets 96
Fisher, Fred 133
Floors 134
frogdesign 105
Furo 54, 108, 116

G

Gehry, Frank 145
Gluck, Peter 89
Gough, Piers 115
Gray, Eileen 42, 149
Gwathmey-Siegel 13

H

Harrods 20
Hastings Tile, Il Bagno 74
Hedborg, Jarrett 59
Hewi 105
Holl, Steven 74, 142
Hollein, Hans 45
Hot Tubs 116
Humpherson, 100
Hurwitz, Sidney 48

I

Indoor-Outdoor Bathrooms 88

J

Jacuzzi 112
James, David 124
Jencks, Charles 48, 84, 115
Jiricna, Eva 42
Joseph 42

K

Kira, Alexander 78, 96, 100
Kroin 124

L

Leyland-Neighlor, Carrie 129
Lighting 122
Losch, Tilly 24
Lustig, Michael 41
Lutyens, Robert 26

M

Marks, Scott 136
Master Bathrooms 62
Maugham, Syrie 26
Mid-State Tile 135
Miller, Herman 59
Mirrors 146
Monzini, Rosanna 143
Moore-Yudell 48
Morphosis 145
Morris, William 150
Moss, Eric 50
Murphy, Brian Alfred 106

N

Nash, Paul 24, 25
Nourrissat, Patrice 67

O

Oakes, George 69
Osburn Design 99, 146
Osterly Castle 101

P

Pantelleria 37
Pawson, John 100
Pinto, Piero 31
Porthault 38, 96

R

Ritter, James 119
Ritz Carlton Hotel 102
Ross, William Post 97

S

Safety 76, 78
Sauvage, Henri 21
Schwartz, Fritz 66
Scurry, Pam 135

Second Bathrooms 84
Shaw, Susanne 119
Sherle Wagner 96
Shire, Peter 132
Short, Yvonne 98
Showers 104
Sinks 96
Small Bathrooms 70
Stamford Hall 27
Steambaths 104
Steele, Eve 32
Stoeltie, R. and B. 28
Storage 140
Sturgis, Simon 115

T

Task Lighting 126
Thermostatic Controls 98
Thorton-Smith, Michael 138
Toilets 100
Tribel 105
Trompe Ploy 128
Tunturi 86
Tye, Alan 76

U

Universal Rundle 81
University of Wisconsin 80

V

Van Deelen, Jerry 126
van der Rohe, Mies 89
Van Royen, Hester 100
Versace, Gianni 46
Villa Fontanella 46
Villino Di Caddi Di Stupinigi 14

W

Walls 128
Walmsey, John 73
Walz, Kevin 127
Wellington-Quigley, Rob 117
Whirlpool Tubs 112
White Allom 26
Windows 150
Windigo Architects 77, 107
Working With A Professional 181
Wright, Frank Lloyd 44

CREDITS

12, Lucinda Lambton/Arcaid
13, Norman McGrath
14, Overseas
14, Lucinda Lambton/Arcaid
15, Lucinda Lambton/Arcaid
16, Overseas
18, Lucinda Lambton/Arcaid
19, Lucinda Lambton/Arcaid
20, Lucinda Lambton/Arcaid
21, Architectural Association
22, Fine Homebuilding
23, Fine Homebuilding
24, Architectural Association
25, Architectural Association
26, National Magazine
26, Country Life
27, National Magazine
28, John Vaughan
28, Fritz von der Schulenburg
29, Maison de Marie Claire/
Berthier/Saconay/Dirand
30, Carla de Benedetti
31, Il Bagno
32, Tim Street-Porter
33, Claude Pataut
34, Overseas
35, Carla de Benedetti
36, Melvyn Bernstein Architects
37, Aldo Ballo
38, Francois Catroux
39, Francois Catroux
40, Jessie Walker
41, Tim Street-Porter
42, Richard Bryant/Arcaid
43, Richard Bryant/Arcaid
45, Il Bagno

45, Jaime Ardiles-Arce
46, Paul Warchol
47, Aldo Ballo
48, Tim Street-Porter
49, Tim Street-Porter
50, Tim Street-Porter/Elizabeth
Whiting & Assoc.
51, Tim Street-Porter
54, Fritz von der Schulenburg/
World of Interiors
54, Maison de Marie Claire/
Korniloff/Hourdin
55, Il Bagno
56, Robert Perron
56, Jessica Strang
57, Robert Perron
57, Claude Pataut
58, Il Bagno
59, Maison de Marie Claire/
Dirand/Chauvel
59, Tim Street-Porter
60, Claude Pataut
61, John Vaughan/World of
Interiors
61, Maison de Marie Claire/
Pataut/Bayle
62, Tim Street-Porter
63, Tim Street-Porter
63, Elizabeth Whiting & Assoc.
64, Maison de Marie Claire/
Korniloff/Hirsch

65, Lucinda Lambton/Arcaid
65, Tom Leighton/World of
Interiors
66, Abitare
66, Maison de Marie Claire/
Korniloff/Hourdin
67, Christian Gervais/Maison
Francaise
68, Elizabeth Whiting & Assoc.
68, Abitare
69, James Mortimer/World of
Interiors
70, Norman McGrath
71, Jessica Strang
71, Aldo Ballo
71, Laura Salvati
72, Laura Salvati
72, Elizabeth Whiting & Assoc.
73, Elizabeth Whiting & Assoc.
73, John Walmsley/Design
Council
74, Steven Holl/Adam Bartos
74, Jessica Strang
74, Richard Bryant/Arcaid
75, Carla de Benedetti
76, Ken Kirkwood/Alen Tye
77, David Arky
78, Jessica Strang
79, Design Council
79, Hewi
80, Dansk Pressalit
81, Universal Rundle
82, Richard Bryant/Arcaid
83, Gabriele Basilico/Abitare
84, Tim Soar/Arcaid
84, Norman McGrath
85, Richard Bryant/Arcaid

86, The Sharper Image Co.
87, Il Bagno
88, Tim Street-Porter
89, Paul Warchol
90, Elizabeth Whiting & Assoc.
91, Brigitte Baert
92, 93, Melvyn Bernstein Arch.
96, D. Porthault
97, William Post Ross/Fine
    Homebuilding
97, John Vaughan
97, Brigitte Baert
97, Robert Perron
98, James Levin
98, Yvonne Short
99, Peter Christenson/Osburn
100, Ken Kirkwood
101, Lucinda Lambton/Arcaid
102, James Levin
103, Il Bagno
104, Jamie Ardiles-Arce
105, Frogdesign
105, Hewi
106, Tim Street-Porter
106, Jens Grundmann/1100 Arch.
107, Il Bagno
107, David Arky, Windigo
108, Il Bagno
109, Kari Haavisto/Yrjo
    Wiherheimo
109, Kari Haavisto/Georg
    Grotenfelt

110, Maison de Marie Claire/
    Halard/Bailbache
111, Elizabeth Whiting & Assoc.
111, Maison de Marie Claire
112, Jeffrey McNamara/Shelton,
    Mindel Associates
113, Aldo Ballo
114, Tim Street-Porter
115, Richard Bryant/Arcaid
116, Robert Perron
116, California Cooperage
117, Tim Street-Porter
118, Ted Brown
119, Susanne Shaw Interiors
122, Robert Perron
122, Maison de Marie Claire/
    Korniloff/Hourdin
123, Maison de Marie Claire
124, Maison de Maire Claire/
    Rozes/Hirsch
124, Tim Street-Porter
125, Aldo Ballo
126, Les Prismatiques
127, Jeffrey McNamara/Shelton,
    Mindel Associates
127, Walz Design
127, Elizabeth Whiting & Assoc.
128, Elizabeth Whiting & Assoc.
128, Tromploy
129, Lucinda Lambton/Arcaid
130, Claude Pataut
130, Elizabeth Whiting & Assoc.
130, M. von Sternberg
131, Il Bagno
132, Tim Street-Porter
133, Tim Street-Porter
134, Brigitte Baert
135, Il Bagno

135, Mid-State Tile
136, R. Giovanni
137, Tim Street-Porter
137, Maison Francaise
138, Robert Perron
138, Michael Thornton-Smith
139, Il Bagno
140, John Vaughan
141, Maison de Marie Claire/
    Pataut/Bayle
141, Elizabeth Whiting & Assoc.
142, Steven Holl/Adam Bartos
142, Jaime Ardiles-Arce
143, Il Bagno
144, Il Bagno
144, Claude Pataut
145, Tim Street-Porter
146, Peter Christenson/Osburn
146, Elizabeth Whiting & Assoc.
147, Tim Street-Porter
147, Elizabeth Whiting & Assoc.
148, Aldo Ballo
149, Rodney Kinsman/G.H.I.
149, Tim Street-Porter
150, Lucinda Lambton/Arcaid
151, Aldo Ballo
151, Brigitte Baert
152, Il Bagno
152, Tim Street-Porter
153, World of Interiors

The personal and professional contributions of many colleagues and friends are woven into this project. However, it is not possible to credit everyone individually, except to say that the lively (and sometimes bemused) response to the subject by so many people added definition to the content, and made assembling this book a truly collaborative effort. Above all I want to express my gratitude to Catherine Revland, Pamela Ferguson, Leslie Fagen, and Debbie Hahn for their generosity of spirit and diligent participation. In addition the following individuals graciously assisted me:
Mark Appleton; Judith Arango; Peter Barna; Scott Carde; Abby Chevalley; Hester Diamond; Barbara Goldstein; Lou Goodman; Nancye Green; Stephen Greengard; Bill Grenewald; James & Kate Gubelmann; Arie Heeres; Craig Jackson; James Hong; Robert Janjigian; Michael Kalil; Archie Kaplan; Keil Erik Killi Olsen; Michele Kolb; Larry Kroin; Hector Leonardi; Fern Mallis; Andrea Marquit; Stephanie Mogavero; David Piscuskas; David Sanders; Lois Sherr; Peter Shire; Horace & Holly Solomon; Judith Stockman; Tim Street-Porter; Jim Tribe; Michelle Vidro; Kevin Walz; Robert Younger; Buzz Yudell.